MAY   1999

Ballymaloe Seasons

Darina Allen

With photographs by
Melanie Eclare, Michelle Garrett,
and Timmy Allen

Roberts Rinehart Publishers

For my father-in-law Ivan Allen who began
it all and encouraged me every step of the way

Ballymaloe Cookery School is run by mega team work, everyone involved with the school contributes to the overall magic in their own way. My thanks go, as ever, to the following people:

To Eileen, Elizabeth, and Haulie who are responsible for the wonderful appearance of the gardens and for the abundance of herbs, fruit, and vegetables throughout the seasons.

To Frank, who nurtures the hens, ducks, and geese and coaxes them to produce lots of eggs and little clutches of chickens and goslings.

To Claire, Iris, Peg, Rachel, Rosemary, Sally, and Sue who teach the students, test recipes, encourage, and cajole and are cheerful through sunny and stormy weather.

To Rosalie, my right hand woman, who has been with me since the beginning, and to Adrienne, who arrived soon after her, both of whom have the unenviable task of organizing my life and keeping me on track, aided and abetted by our receptionist Cathriona.

To Mary and Bessie who pamper and spoil me; to Eleanor who composes poetry as she irons; and to Ber and her team who get the cottages looking fresh and lovely for each new group of students or guests and put a little garden posy of flowers in each room.

To Marie and Doreen who keep us sparkling and to the ever-smiling Grainne who does just about everything with great humor.

To Will and his building team who seem to manage to create everything from follies to cafés with the minimum of direction and the motto "no problem."

To all my family: my parents-in-law, Ivan and Myrtle, ever an inspiration, ever supportive; my mother Elizabeth O'Connell, who encouraged me every step of the way; my brother Rory O'Connell, chef at Ballymaloe House, who shares his creativity with me; and to my children, Isaac, Toby, Lydia, and Emily, who have inherited a wild and crazy mother—their smiles and hugs make it all worth the effort.

And, last but not least, to my dear Tim who has endured my flights of fancy for more than 26 years now.

This book is a celebration of all their efforts.

Darina Allen and the Publishers would like to thank the Bank of Ireland for the generous help with the photography contained in this book.

Contents

A Note on Ingredients 6

Introduction 8

Spring 12
Introduction 13
First Courses 20
Main Courses 28
Vegetables 38
Desserts 42

Summer 50
Introduction 51
First Courses 58
Main Courses 68
Vegetables 78
Desserts 86

Autumn 96
Introduction 97
First Courses 104
Main Courses 114
Vegetables 126
Desserts 132

Winter 140
Introduction 141
First Courses 156
Main Courses 166
Vegetables 164
Desserts 170

Basics recipes 182

Index 190

Photographic
acknowledgements 192

A Note on Ingredients

Our gardens produce endless delights for us through the year and every season brings its own rewards. I will never forget the year that Timmy ambled in asking, 'Have you looked at your almond tree recently?' I was wild with excitement when I discovered the first soft, furry, green almonds. Now we have a little almond feast every year.

Quite apart from depending on the wealth of food from our gardens, much of our work at the School would be impossible without the support of our local producers. Take the Irish farmhouse cheese makers for instance, who provide a gorgeous array of delicious produce. Most of them are women, with a few exceptions, and they are a charismatic lot—free spirited and passionate about their craft. I feel truly grateful to these artisans who are prepared to spend long hours making and nurturing their cheese to ensure that each cheese develops to its full potential. So try one of the many varieties they produce from cow, goat and ewe's milk—Milleens, Gubbeen, Durrus, Cashel Blue, Baylough, Desmond, Croghan, Orla, Ardsallagh, Knocklara, Kerry, Cooleeney, Coolea, Abbey Blue, Killorglin, Chetwynd, Ardrahan, Lavistown, Ring, Boilie... there are over 80 to choose from.

It is really good to be demanding of the important basics in your kitchen. Good quality salt, pepper and oil are incredibly important because they are used in most dishes; careless use of poor quality goods will spoil even the most robust meal. Therefore choose these ingredients carefully.

Salt: we use plain dairy salt in our cooking which has no additives that may mar the flavor of your food. On the table, we use Maldon sea salt or hand-panned sea salt from Brittany.

Pepper: use peppercorns and grind them specially for each dish. Ideally have one mill for black and one for white. They vary enormously so hunt around for really aromatic ones.

Oil: virtually everything sold under the title of 'cooking oil' is of poor quality. Buy good quality sunflower, peanut or pure olive oil for frying and extra virgin oil for dressings, pesto and drizzling.

Vinegar: malt vinegar is fine for pickles and chutneys but wine vinegars, especially wood-aged ones, make a great difference to your recipes. Make your own infused vinegars and oils (see page 184)—they are so easy to prepare and infinitely less expensive than the attractively packaged bottles on the specialist food shelves.

Eggs: the quality of eggs makes a phenomenal difference to the flavor of even the most simple dishes. Always use free-range; better still, if you live in the country, get a few hens! They will eat your scraps and reward you with delicious eggs.

Sugar: soft brown Barbados sugar sprinkled over porridge, apple tart or yoghurt magically transforms these staple foods.

Honey: the number of different flavored honeys you can get is a revelation. The taste is affected by the flowers from which the bees collect their pollen. Our local honey is predominantly apple blossom, heather or mixed flowers from west Cork.

Chocolate: choose brands with a high percentage of cocoa solids—we use Valrhona, Lesmé, Meunier, Suchard and Lindt.

Cream: Irish dairy products are still superb quality. The cream that we get from our local creamery is essentially heavy cream (about 42% butterfat). Thin cream whips softly but heavy cream is the richest and has the best flavor. Use sparingly.

Butter: we use both salted and unsalted Irish butter; the flavor is wonderful.

The success of the recipes in this book depends upon sourcing really good, naturally produced ingredients so be a fussy shopper and remember that there is no point in buying or growing organically produced food and then boiling the hell out of it!

7

Introduction

During my last year at school, I was agonizing about which career path to follow. It was a toss up between Hotel Management, Cooking, and Horticulture. Cooking, which was my real love, wasn't considered quite posh enough then, in the mid-sixties, so I opted for a Hotel and Catering Management course at Cathal Brugha Street, as the Dublin Hotel School was known at that time. This lively, vibrant school was run by several deeply committed, matriarchal women of whom one was Mór Murnaghan.

Toward the end of the course, most of my friends had organized management jobs, but I was frantically trying to get into one of the top restaurant kitchens. Good restaurants were few and far between in Ireland then, and I soon discovered that none of them was interested in having a woman in the kitchen—women still cooked at home or in cafés, men were real chefs!

I told Mór one day that I longed to find a job that involved cooking with fresh food and making homemade ice cream and breads, cooking with the seasons: not an unreasonable request nowadays, but back then this was a tall order. As luck would have it, Mór had just been to a dinner party where the conversation centered around an extraordinary development—a farmer's wife down in the wilds of East Cork had opened a restaurant in her old country house. She wrote the menu every day based on what was available in the locality, in the garden and greenhouse, and from the local fishermen at Ballycotton. This woman was Myrtle Allen, who is now my mother-in-law.

Myrtle gave her guests the kind of food that she cooked for family and friends, and they loved it—real food with real flavor, simply cooked.

Timmy Allen, Myrtle and Ivan's long-haired eldest son, was the first person I met when I drove up the long winding avenue to Ballymaloe. He ran up, barefoot and in shorts, from the beginnings of the golf course, to greet me: "Are you the person who is coming to help?" Little did he know that his fate was sealed! Even though he took no notice of me for most of the summer, as he entertained one lovely girlfriend after the other, winter eventually came and I was still there. We married in 1970 and moved into Kinoith, the lovely Regency house given to Timmy by his parents who had inherited it from a gentle Quaker, Wilson Strangman. It had the wild remains of an old garden and some crumbling outbuildings. We were very young and soon had several lovely children. Timmy was farming, but it was really quite difficult to make any reasonable living from horticulture at that time. We seemed to get less for our beautiful produce every year. We ran a fantastic farm shop beside the greenhouses, a seven-day-a-week job, very rewarding but equally hard work, and in reality the season was too short to make it really worthwhile.

(ABOVE) *Sorrel can be used to make wonderful salads and soups. It may taste strong to some people so, all recipes that use it can be made with half lettuce/half sorrel for a milder flavor. We grow Buckler's leaf sorrel* (Rumex scutatus) *and common, or broad leafed sorrel,* (Rumex acetosa).

At Ballymaloe House, business was quiet during the winter months, so Myrtle gave cooking classes. I assisted her as she became busier. She suggested that I teach some classes, and eventually I picked up courage and put an ad in the *Cork Examiner*. Much to my astonishment, people came. I gave cooking classes on Saturday mornings in the kitchen of the White Cottage at Kinoith, starting with about ten students, and they really seemed to enjoy it.

As a very special treat, Timmy gave me a present of a cookery course with Marcella Hazan in Bologna. It was an extremely expensive course. I couldn't dream of telling anyone what it cost, but, with hindsight, it was possibly the best investment we've ever made. There in Italy, as Marcella and Victor Hazan waxed lyrical about the food and wine of their beloved country, I suddenly realized the quality of the produce I had at home, on our farm, in our garden and in the greenhouses, and in our local markets.

I arrived home "born again," convinced that I should open a cookery school right there on our farm. I chatted with Timmy and my parents-in-law. We decided we would convert some of the farm buildings beside our house. I was still feeding our younger daughter, Emily, so it seemed the way forward. We went along to see the bank manager, who listened intently to my grand plans. No doubt he couldn't believe his ears! Needless to say, I had nothing but gut-feeling to back up my theory. To my astonishment he pronounced that it was "a complete non-runner" and he was sorry to dampen enthusiasm, but…

I came home crestfallen. My parents-in-law couldn't bear my disappointment, so they decided to take a gamble and act as guarantor. Their suggestion that I call the new venture "Ballymaloe Cookery School" was even more touching and supportive. It was a tremendous boost and made me more determined to live up to the Ballymaloe reputation. The Ballymaloe Cookery School opened its newly painted doors in September, 1983. From the start we offered both long and short courses, hoping to attract hobby cooks and would-be professionals.

Within a short time, food writers and journalists who came to Ballymaloe wandered over to Kinoith, just 2 miles away, to check out the new venture, and they seemed to like what they found. Within two years we had students from the U. S., Australia, and Denmark. Soon we were bursting at the seams. Timmy suggested converting the old apple house, a much larger building across the yard. I thought it was far too big, but he was absolutely right: we jumped from taking 18 students up to 38 in 1996, and now we take 44. There's one teacher with every six students, and Timmy now teaches at the School. Despite the demand we don't intend to get any bigger; there's a great atmosphere and we can keep in touch with all our students and help them to get jobs, answer their queries, and have lots of chats with them.

(BELOW) *We are lucky enough to have many glorious types of campanulas in several colors — blues, purples, and whites are the most common. Campanulas grow very easily if they like your soil. These Queen Elizabeth roses also make a spectacular show in the summer months.*

The gardens, once a wilderness, have gradually been restored over the years. It seemed logical to develop them even further to produce our own herbs, vegetables, fruit, and honey, and this has proved a major attraction for both students and journalists. For me, gardening is now as much of a passion as cooking.

The herb garden, which we designed in 1989, was originally drawn up on the back of an envelope after a visit to Villandry in the Loire Valley in France. A vegetable *potager*, formal fruit garden, water garden, pond garden, shell house, and Celtic maze have followed. Each year a new folly…

It's wonderful to watch the gardens develop. We were so fortunate to inherit the original gardens, that I feel I want to create something lasting and special to pass on to the next generation, in gratitude for the many wonderful trees and plants that the Strangman family planted and that we now enjoy.

Cooking here, too, developing new ideas and experimenting with different ingredients, now so abundantly available from all over the world, is hugely enjoyable. I am spoiled and get the chance to travel, and, of course, through my television work, there has come a huge range of contacts and chances to chat over ideas about ways of combining various ingredients. Interaction is vital to inspire development and change.

The seasons and the students are the joy of Ballymaloe Cookery School.

Spring

Once I've found the first snowdrop under the beech trees down by the pond, I know that Spring is around the corner; we have a particularly early variety given to me by the mother of Hazel, my sister-in-law. There are wonderful double snowdrops, which have survived since the Strangmans lived in this house and created the garden in the 1830s. I bet they did not consider that the snowdrops would still be cheering the wild and crazy woman who has inherited their garden so many years later.

Ballymaloe Cookery School wakes up in the New Year with the first of our two three-month certificate courses, when some 44 keen students arrive full of excitement and fill the cottages in our courtyard, eager to learn, yet a little apprehensive on the first day. We always say a little silent prayer that the weather will be nice that day. One of the first things they do is visit the greenhouses and the vegetable garden—and I see immediately how bereft the garden is of produce. We pick the kale, sometimes known as "cut-and-come" and "hungry gap" because it provides an endless supply of

dark green vegetable when there is little else fresh. Our staff of 26 is made up of many ex-students who've married local people, so our contribution has been to bring a bit of new blood into the area!

The approach of spring promises new vegetables and fruits. Fresh green watercress and tender nettles and sorrel appear, and the slightly wary students learn to make delicious, iron-rich soups. I got terracotta seakale and rhubarb forcing pots from Whichford Pottery in England, so now we can have supplies in time for the salmon season, shortly after St. Patrick's Day. The little chives start pushing through the soil and we add the flowers to our salads, making a glorious dash of rich purple and white. We have lots of corn salad and the deeply serrated oriental green, mysticana, to liven up the early spring salads. I love the clean taste of the February citrus fruits—the pink grapefruits from Texas, the blood oranges from Spain, and clementines, mandarins, and ugli fruits, so good and versatile when they are in season. Of course we make marmalade—I adore the smell of marmalade cooking. We make our own bread every day, all year round, lovely sourdough breads and yeast breads. I hope it is true to say that none of the students goes away from the School without a thorough knowledge of breadmaking skills and the immense pleasure to be had from baking. Who can forget the wonderful smells that waft from the oven when a loaf is just baked to perfection?

Some of the land around here has never been turned in living memory. It is full of many different kinds of wild grasses, wild herbs, and flowers that come up in the springtime; quite lovely. Michael Cuddigan, our third- or fourth-generation traditional butcher from Cloyne, buys cattle raised on these pastures; they have more flavor than the ones raised in fields with just two or three grasses to eat. Mr. Cuddigan provides our meat for the School and Ballymaloe House. We make big cassoulets and stews at this time, flavored with herbs from the garden. One vegetable after another starts to appear, and from having so little at the beginning of Spring, we are suddenly faced with variety—so many good things you simply cannot harvest them fast enough.

(LEFT) *Ballymaloe Cookery School is 800 yards from the Atlantic Ocean and benefits from the huge wealth of saltwater fish landed at the fishing village, Ballycotton, nearby.*

(RIGHT) *The ten to twelve varieties of chicken provide free-range eggs for the School.*

The ducklings hatch! Out come the proud mothers, each with 8 or 10 ducklings in tow. Frank Walsh, who looks after them and all the chickens that roam the gardens, is proud as Punch. There are many rare breeds of chicken at Ballymaloe Cookery School—they scratch in the yard and lay the vast numbers of eggs used by the students each week. Timmy does the marketing and the provisioning, visiting the marvelous market in Cork City on Wednesdays and coming back laden with goodies. It's a covered market, with a labyrinth of lanes, behind St. Patrick's Street, the workplace for third- and fourth-generation traders. Alongside them are hippies and the new generation of stallholders. It is possible to buy anything from pigs' tails, skirts, and bodices (cuts of pork) to tripe and drisheen (blood sausage). Toby Simmonds sells 15 or 20 different types of olives. There are breads of every sort, game, chickens, and buttered (preserved) eggs. I love the banter with the stallholders, and bring every group of students here because there are foods for sale in that market that would be impossible to get anywhere else in the world.

(ABOVE) *The hall of the Cookery School is where we greet the students when they first arrive. The chairs are made by my son, Isaac.*

(RIGHT) *The chickens are totally free-range and wander everywhere about the School gardens.*

(FAR RIGHT) *The Muscovy ducks and the geese are beautiful birds; their purpose is mainly ornamental, but they do keep the snails at bay.*

The tiny daffodils burst into flower in the fruit garden, underplanted with spring bulbs to cheer me up in the dreary weeks of February and March. Now we have crocus, *Iris reticulata*, winter snowflakes. The hellebore bed is a triumph. Someone kindly gave me a huge gift token for Carewswood Garden Centre, and I blitzed the whole lot on hellebores, 10 or 12 kinds. Fortunately they love that spot under the fruit garden wall, outside the Cookery School window, and we will plant lots of snowdrops in the gaps next year. We have incredibly fragrant little violets, so beautiful and so much a portent of spring, which must have been planted by the Strangmans and which I collected out of the ditches. We make sensationally pretty crystallized violets in the School.

Easter comes and the three-month course, exhausting as it is exhilarating, finishes up with the tension of the exams. The students and the staff go off to well-earned breaks, and we celebrate with glorious Easter lamb, served with fresh

(ABOVE) *The snake's head fritillaria* (Fritillaria meleagris) *has a characteristic freckling, which does not appear on the white form, "Aphrodite." At Ballymaloe they contrast beautifully with the miniature daffodils at Eastertime.*

(BELOW) *The fruit garden is underplanted with many spring flowers; among them various crocuses, tulips, and daphnes.*

(ABOVE) Vibernum Bodnantense *flowers in the very early spring and has the most delicate fragrance. It lasts extremely well as a cut flower and perfumes the entire room.*

mint—I use spearmint for the best flavor, though we grow five or six different varieties. There are the decorated eggs and we have picnics—it's in my blood: my mother, Elizabeth O'Connell, once took all nine of her children on a wonderful picnic to the top of Cullohill Mountain on Christmas Day. I make the Simnel Cake on Easter Monday and then toast it so it's still fresh on our picnics—divine with cups of Barry's tea. We take sausages; our son, Isaac, lights a fire and they are cooked in the little black tin pan that has done service for so many years. We picnic at a special place just beside the river Dissour at Easter, where there are beds of wild garlic and wood anemones in bloom. Quite magical.

Wild Garlic Soup

SERVES 6

4 tablespoons butter
2 cups peeled and diced potatoes
1 cup diced onions
2 cups chopped wild garlic (bulbs and
leaves)
1 teaspoon salt
Freshly ground black pepper
5 cups Homemade Chicken
Stock (see page 184)
About ¹/₂ cup cream or half-and-half

GARNISH
Wild garlic flowers

In late April, the air at the top of Wilson's Wood is heavy with the smell of wild garlic. The pretty white flowers mix with the bluebells and primroses. Both the bulbs and leaves of wild garlic (Allium vineale) are used to flavor this delicious soup. Dig the bulbs up, don't pull them. The flowers look beautiful sprinkled over the top of the bowls of soup.

Melt the butter in a heavy saucepan. When it foams, add the potatoes, onions, and wild garlic, and toss in the butter until well coated. Sprinkle with salt and pepper. Cover and sweat on low heat for 10 minutes. Add the stock and cook until the vegetables are soft.

Purée the soup in a blender or food processor, then taste and adjust the seasoning. Add a little cream to taste. Serve hot, sprinkled with a few wild garlic flowers.

Spring Cabbage Soup with Crispy Seaweed

SERVES 6

4 tablespoons butter
I cup peeled and chopped potatoes
³/₄ cup chopped onions
Salt and freshly ground black pepper
3³/₄ cups light Homemade
Chicken Stock (see page 184)
3¹/₂ cups chopped young spring cabbage
leaves (stems removed)
¹/₄ – ¹/₂ cup cream or half-and-half

CRISPY SEAWEED
Savoy cabbage
Oil for frying
Salt
Sugar

The idea of cabbage soup may not thrill you, but just try this one. Use the freshest, greenest cabbage and take great care not to overcook it. Cook and eat, don't reheat! The Crispy Seaweed can be used as a garnish or served separately, as an appetizer.

Melt the butter in a heavy pan. When it foams, add the potatoes and onions and turn them in the butter until well coated. Sprinkle with salt and pepper. Cover and sweat on low heat for 10 minutes. Add the stock (heat it first if you want to speed things up) and cook until the potatoes are soft. Add the cabbage and cook, uncovered, until the cabbage is just cooked—a matter of 4–5 minutes. Keeping the lid off retains the green color.

To make the Crispy Seaweed, remove the outer leaves from the cabbage and cut out the stalks. Roll the leaves into cigar shapes and slice across into the thinnest possible shreds with a very sharp knife. Heat the oil in a deep-fryer to 350°F. Toss in some cabbage and cook for just a few seconds. As soon as it starts to crisp, remove and drain on paper towels. Sprinkle with salt and sugar. Toss, and serve as a garnish on the soup or just nibble: it's quite addictive—worse than peanuts or popcorn!

Purée the soup in a blender or food processor. Taste and adjust the seasoning. Add the cream before serving. Serve alone or with a mound of Crispy Seaweed on top.

Potato, Scallion, and Tarragon Soup with Crusty Breadsticks

We make this soup with the first fresh tarragon of spring, when the potatoes are beginning to get old. Crusty Breadsticks are delicious with it, but, of course, you can eat them with any soup. The more rustic-looking they are, the better.

SERVES 6

Ballymaloe White Yeast Bread dough (see page 180)
Coarse salt, cumin seeds, or freshly chopped rosemary to sprinkle

SOUP
4 tablespoons butter
3 cups peeled and diced potatoes
1 cup chopped scallions (we use both the white and the green parts)
1 teaspoon salt
Freshly ground black pepper
2–3 teaspoons chopped fresh French tarragon
3 1/2 cups Homemade Chicken Stock (see page 184)
1/2 cup half-and-half

GARNISH
Fresh tarragon

Preheat the oven to 450°F.

When the dough has been punched down, let it rest for a few minutes. Sprinkle the work surface with coarse salt, cumin seeds, or freshly chopped rosemary. Pull off small pieces of dough, each about 1/2 ounce in weight. Cover the rest of the dough while you work with one piece. Roll each one into a thin breadstick, brush with a tiny drop of oil, and roll the sticks individually in the salt, seeds, or herbs until they are well coated. Place on a baking sheet and bake for 10–15 minutes or until golden brown and crisp. Cool on a wire rack. (Breadsticks are usually baked without a final rising, but, for a slightly lighter result, let the shaped dough rise for about 10 minutes before baking.)

Melt the butter in a heavy saucepan. When it foams, add the potatoes and the scallions and toss them in the butter until well coated. Sprinkle with salt and pepper. Cover and sweat on low heat for 8–10 minutes. Add the chopped tarragon and the stock. Cook until the vegetables are just soft, then purée the soup in a blender. Taste and adjust the seasoning. Thin with half-and-half to the desired consistency. Serve hot, sprinkled with a little snipped tarragon.

Carpaccio with Slivers of Parmesan, Arugula, and Truffle Oil

SERVES 12

A 1-pound beef tenderloin roast (fresh not frozen)
Fresh arugula, about 5 leaves per person
4–5 very thin slivers Parmesan cheese per person (Parmigiano Reggiano is best)
Sea salt and freshly ground black pepper
Truffle oil or extra virgin olive oil

Many people feel uneasy about eating raw beef, but we have no such qualms because we are fortunate in having an excellent butcher.

Chill the meat, then slice it as thinly as possible with a very sharp knife. Place each slice on a piece of oiled plastic wrap and cover with a second piece. Roll gently with a rolling pin until the meat is almost transparent and has doubled in size. Peel the plastic wrap off the top, invert the meat onto a chilled plate, and gently peel away the other piece of plastic wrap.

Put the arugula leaves on top of the beef and scatter with very thin slivers of Parmesan. Sprinkle with sea salt and pepper. Or, pile the beef on top of the arugula. Drizzle with truffle oil or with extra virgin olive oil and serve immediately with crusty bread—ciabatta and focaccia (see page 178) are best.

Deep-Fried Sprats with Aïoli

SERVES 6–8

AIOLI

I–4 cloves garlic, depending on size
Pinch of English mustard powder or
$^1/_4$ teaspoon Dijon mustard
Salt and freshly ground black pepper
2 egg yolks, preferably free-range
I cup oil (either sunflower,
groundnut, peanut, or olive, or a
mixture)
2 teaspoons white wine vinegar

Oil for deep-frying
I pound fresh sprats
All-purpose flour seasoned with salt and
pepper
Lemon wedges
Oyster shells (optional) for serving

GARNISH
2 teaspoons chopped parsley

In general, January has few highlights, apart from the arrival of the Seville oranges for marmalade. When the sprats arrive in Ballycotton, however, the excitement is tremendous. We feast on them (deep-fried, soused, pickled, and smoked) for a few short weeks. We don't even think of eviscerating them; you may be shocked, but we eat them insides and all! For our oil mixture we use 3 parts peanut oil to 1 part olive oil.

First make the aïoli. Using a mortar and pestle, work the garlic with a little salt and pepper until smooth; then work in the mustard and egg yolks. Add the wine vinegar and the oil drop by drop, stirring constantly with the pestle. Once the sauce has started to thicken, the rest of the oil can be added more quickly. Stir in the chopped parsley.

Alternatively, use a food processor to purée the garlic, mustard, egg yolks and seasoning. With the blades still turning, add the oil in a thin stream. Add the vinegar at the end.

Taste the aïoli and add a few drops of fresh lemon juice, salt, and pepper, if necessary. Just before serving, heat oil in a deep-fryer to 400°F. Toss the sprats in well-seasoned flour and fry until crisp and golden. Serve immediately with wedges of lemon garnished with parsley. An oyster shell on each plate holds a generous spoonful of aïoli perfectly.

Smoked Irish Salmon with Potato Wafers and Horseradish Mayonnaise

SERVES 6

4 large potatoes
Olive oil (or a mixture of olive and
sunflower oil) for deep-frying
Salt
Horseradish Mayonnaise (see page 186)
18 slices smoked salmon
Freshly squeezed lemon juice
Freshly ground black pepper

GARNISH
Red onion rings, sprinkled with vinegar
and sugar
Fresh chives

I ate this first in a restaurant in California, made with lox and presented as a crisp high pile. The waiters managed to move around without it toppling!

Scrub the potatoes and cut into very thin slices, preferably using a mandoline. Heat the oil in a deep-fryer and cook the potato slices until crisp and golden. Drain on paper towels. Season with salt.

Prepare the Horseradish Mayonnaise.

To assemble: Put a little Mayonnaise in the center of a plate, with a warm potato wafer on top and a ruffle of smoked salmon on top of that. Brush with freshly squeezed lemon juice, then add another blob of Mayonnaise, some pepper, and another potato wafer. Repeat twice more if you can manage to balance it, ending with a potato wafer. Garnish with more Horseradish Mayonnaise, red onion rings, and a couple of cheeky chives.

Warm Salad of Lamb Kidneys, Straw Potatoes, and Caramelized Shallots

SERVES 4

About 4 generous handfuls of a selection
of salad greens (butterhead lettuce,
Red Leaf lettuce, curly endive, romaine,
watercress, arugula, etc.)

FOR THE DRESSING
6 tablespoons olive oil
2 tablespoons white wine vinegar
1/4 teaspoon Dijon mustard
Salt and freshly ground black pepper
A pinch sugar

20 Caramelized Shallots (see below)

FOR THE STRAW POTATOES
I large potato (4–6 ounces)
Oil for deep-frying

2 tablespoons olive oil
4 lamb kidneys, trimmed of all fat and
gristle and cut into 1/2-inch dice
Salt and freshly ground black pepper
I tablespoon freshly chopped marjoram

GARNISH
Fresh majoram sprigs

The variety meats from spring lamb are so tender. We feast on lamb kidneys when the lambs are young. Our butcher, Mr. Cuddigan, keeps his own herd on herb-filled pastures, with delicious results.

Wash and dry the salad greens, tear into bite-sized pieces, and keep in a salad bowl. Whisk together the ingredients for the dressing and set aside. Prepare and cook the Caramelized Shallots.

Peel the potato and cut into fine julienne strips on a mandoline, in a food processor, or by hand. Rinse off excess starch with cold water, drain, and pat dry. Heat oil in a deep-fryer to 400°F. Fry the potatoes until golden brown and crisp. Keep them warm to serve with the salad.

Just before serving, heat the olive oil in a skillet until very hot. Season the kidneys with salt and pepper, add to the pan, and cook until done to your taste. Sprinkle with chopped marjoram. Don't overcook the kidneys or they will become tough and rubbery. While the kidneys are cooking, toss the salad greens quickly with the dressing and divide among the plates. Put the warm shallots around each pile of salad, and arrange the Straw Potatoes carefully on top of each shallot in a little pile. Finally, sprinkle the cooked kidneys straight from the pan onto the salads. Garnish with tiny sprigs of majoram and serve immediately.

Caramelized Shallots

SERVES 4

I pound peeled shallots
4 tablespoons butter
1/2 cup water
I–2 tablespoons sugar
Salt and freshly ground black pepper
Sprig of fresh thyme or rosemary

Serve these with Warm Salad of Lamb Kidneys (see above), steaks, fish, or a mixture of roasted vegetables (see page 168).

Put all of the ingredients into a saucepan. Bring to a boil, then let simmer, covered, until the shallots are almost tender. Remove the lid and allow the juices to evaporate. Watch and turn carefully as the shallots begin to caramelize.

Asparagus on Buttered Toast

SERVES 4

16–20 fresh asparagus spears
4 slices of very fresh bread, preferably
Ballymaloe White Yeast Bread, (see
page 180)
Butter

Hollandaise Sauce (see page 182)

GARNISH
Freshly chopped chervil

Of all the ways I have eaten asparagus, this is my absolute favorite.

Trim off the coarse end of the asparagus and peel the stalks. Save the trimmings for soup.

Make the Hollandaise Sauce and keep warm.

Just before serving, cook the asparagus in boiling salted water. If you have a special asparagus kettle, that's wonderful, but you can manage very well without one. Depending upon the thickness of the spears, the asparagus will take 4–8 minutes to cook. Test by putting the tip of a sharp knife through the thicker end; it should go through easily. Remove the spears from the water and drain.

Toast the bread slices and butter them while they are still warm. (Cut off the crusts if you must, but the bread is so good that I leave them on.) Divide the asparagus among the slices and top with a few spoonfuls of Hollandaise. Garnish with freshly chopped chervil and eat immediately.

Goat Cheese Crostini with Balsamic Onions and Watercress

SERVES 4

6 ounces fresh goat cheese
Salt and freshly ground black pepper
$1/2$ cup cream, softly whipped
$1/2$ teaspoon chopped fresh thyme
$1/4$ teaspoon chopped fresh rosemary
2 tablespoons olive oil
2 cups sliced onions
Balsamic vinegar

Bunch of watercress, trimmed and washed

FOR THE CROSTINI
4 slices white country bread, or 8 slices
ciabatta or French baguette cut at an angle
Extra virgin olive oil

Our goat cheese comes from a herd owned by Erwin and Ina Korner near Youghal, in County Cork. The goats live a very happy life. The cheese made from their milk is soft, so try to find an equivalent, very fresh, goat cheese for this recipe.

Press the goat cheese through a strainer into a bowl. Season with salt and pepper, and fold in the softly whipped cream and chopped herbs. Cover and refrigerate until needed. Heat 1 tablespoon of olive oil in a sauté pan. Toss in the sliced onions and sweat until almost soft and lightly caramelized. Add the balsamic vinegar and cook for 2–3 minutes longer. Set aside.

Heat enough olive oil to cover the bottom of a skillet to a depth of 1 inch until the oil is almost smoking. Cook the bread on both sides until pale golden. Drain on paper towels.

Preheat the broiler or a hot oven. Spread a generous amount of goat cheese cream on the crostini and pop under the broiler or into the oven. Strip the watercress leaves from the main stem and toss the leaves in a little extra virgin olive oil and a few drops of balsamic vinegar. Season with salt and pepper. Put the crostini on a bed of watercress, with a few balsamic onion rings sprinkled around the edge. Serve immediately.

Chargrilled Scallops with Eggplant and Pesto

SERVES 4

1–2 eggplants
Salt and freshly ground black pepper
Pesto (see page 186)
Olive oil
12–16 sea scallops

GARNISH
Fresh basil leaves

I tasted this combination in Cantina, a restaurant in London, and I was so excited that I wrote about it for the Irish Times *when I got back home. We get our scallops from Kenmare Bay, but wherever you get yours make sure that they are big, plump, and sweet.*

Slice the eggplant lengthwise into ¼ inch thick slices, sprinkle with salt, and let drain for 15–20 minutes.

Meanwhile, make the pesto (or use a jar of good-quality, ready-made pesto). Rinse the eggplant slices and pat dry with paper towels. Brush with a little olive oil and, over charcoal or on a very hot ridged cast-iron grill pan, cook quickly on both sides. Just before serving, season the scallops with salt and freshly ground pepper, then grill them. (A nonstick skillet also gives a very good result.) Let them brown well on one side before turning them over.

To serve, cover each plate with eggplant slices, arrange three or four scallops on top, and drizzle a little pesto between the scallops and eggplant slices. Garnish with a sprig of fresh basil and serve immediately.

Panfried Scallops with Beurre Blanc

SERVES 4 (OR 8 AS A FIRST COURSE)

12 large sea scallops
Salt and freshly ground black pepper

BEURRE BLANC
3 tablespoons white wine
3 tablespoons white wine vinegar
1 tablespoon minced shallots
Salt and freshly ground white pepper
2 tablespoons heavy cream
$^3/_4$ cup (1$^1/_2$ sticks) cold unsalted
butter, cut into small cubes
Freshly squeezed lemon juice

GARNISH
Fresh fennel or chervil sprigs

This is the most exquisite way to eat really fresh scallops. Some people may feel beurre blanc appears everywhere these days, but this is still the most sublime combination of flavors.

First make the Beurre Blanc. Put the wine, wine vinegar, shallots, and a little pepper into a heavy stainless-steel saucepan. Boil to reduce to about $^1/_2$ tablespoon. Add the cream and boil again until it thickens. Whisk in the cold butter, a few cubes at a time, keeping the sauce just warm enough to absorb the butter. Strain out the shallots, and season with salt, white pepper, and lemon juice. Keep warm in a bowl set over hot but not simmering water or in a double boiler.

Just before serving, slice each scallop in half to get two rounds of equal thickness. Dry on paper towels. Season the scallops with salt and pepper. Heat a nonstick skillet and put in the scallops in a single layer, not too close together. Cook on one side until golden before turning them over to cook the other side.

Spoon a little very thin Beurre Blanc onto a large hot plate for each person (thin the sauce if necessary by whisking in warm water). Arrange the slices of scallop on top of the sauce, garnish with fennel or chervil, and serve immediately.

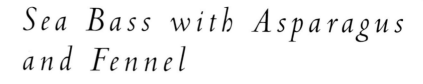

Sea Bass with Asparagus and Fennel

SERVES 6

6 pieces of sea bass fillet, 6 ounces each, scaled but not skinned
Sea salt and freshly ground white pepper
12 fresh asparagus spears
Extra virgin olive oil
I Florence fennel bulb, trimmed and cut into diagonal slices
Colonna Granverde (lemon-flavored olive oil)

GARNISH
Fennel leaves

Try to dovetail the cooking of the asparagus, fresh fish, and fennel so that everything is ready to serve at almost the same moment.

Preheat the oven to 450°F; prepare a charcoal fire or heat a ridged cast-iron grill pan.

Trim the asparagus and peel the root end thinly with a swivel-top peeler. Drizzle with a little extra virgin olive oil, toss gently to coat, and season with sea salt. Roast in the preheated oven for 8–10 minutes.

Score the fillets quite deeply on the skin-side to prevent them from curling. Season with salt and pepper. Heat a thin film of olive oil in a nonstick skillet to just below smoking point. Place the fillets, skin-side down, in the skillet and cook for 2–3 minutes, until a nice crust forms. Turn the fillets over and complete cooking in the preheated oven—about 5–8 minutes, depending on their thickness.

Drizzle the fennel with extra virgin olive oil and turn gently to coat. Season with salt and pepper. Grill for 1–2 minutes on each side.

Arrange each piece of fish, skin-side up, on a hot plate. Drizzle a little Colonna Granverde over the fish. Surround with the roasted asparagus, cut into smaller pieces at an angle, and slices of chargrilled fennel. Garnish with a few feathery fennel leaves and eat immediately.

Wild Irish Salmon with Seakale

SERVES 6

I center-cut piece of fresh wild salmon, weighing 2¹/₂ pounds
Salt (use I heaping tablespoon to every 5 cups of water)

Hollandaise Sauce (see page 182)

Seakale (see page 38)

GARNISH
Fennel leaves

Salmon, seakale, and Hollandaise Sauce—a marriage made in heaven. But if a small piece of fish is cooked in a large amount of water, much of the flavor will escape into the water, so I use the smallest pan possible. Needless to say, I never poach a salmon steak because the maximum surface is exposed to the water, resulting in maximum loss of flavor.

First poach the salmon. The proportion of salt to water is very important. Choose a pan that will fit the fish exactly. Half fill the pan with the measured salted water and bring to a boil. Put in the fish, cover, bring back to a boil, and simmer gently for 20 minutes. Remove from the heat and let the fish sit in the water for no longer than 5–8 minutes. Meanwhile, make the Hollandaise Sauce and cook the seakale.

Remove the fish from the poaching liquid. Remove the skin and divide the fish into portions, being careful to remove all bones. Garnish with fennel leaves and serve hot with the sauce, seakale, and some new potatoes.

Roasted Cod or Hake with Crispy Onions and Parsley Pesto

SERVES 6

Tomato Fondue (see page 182)
Parsley Pesto (see page 186)
Crispy Onions (see page 188)
6 pieces of cod or hake fillet, 6 ounces
each, with skin
Extra virgin olive oil
Salt and freshly ground white pepper

GARNISH

Fresh flat-leaf parsley or chervil leaves

For this recipe you need to use thick fillet from a large fish. It is vital to leave the skin on and to use very fresh fish.

Preheat the oven to 450°F.

Prepare the Tomato Fondue, Parsley Pesto, and Crispy Onions.

Score the fish skin quite deeply to prevent it from curling. Heat a thin film of extra virgin olive oil in a nonstick skillet to just under smoking point. Season the fish and place, skin-side down, in the skillet. Cook until a nice crust forms. Turn the pieces of fish over and complete the cooking skin-side up in the oven.

To serve, put a piece of roasted fish, skin-side uppermost, on a hot plate. Garnish the plate with two dollops each of Tomato Fondue, Parsley Pesto, and Crispy Onions. Sprinkle with parsley or chervil leaves. Drizzle with extra virgin olive oil and serve immediately, because the skin loses its crispness quite quickly.

Deh-Ta Hsiung's Steamed Striped Mullet

SERVES ABOUT 6

1 striped mullet (sea bass could be used instead), scaled, trimmed, and cleaned
1 teaspoon salt
1 teaspoon Asian sesame oil
4 scallions
2–3 dried Chinese mushrooms, soaked and thinly shredded
$^1/_2$ cup thinly shredded pork tenderloin or cooked ham
2 tablespoons light soy sauce
1 tablespoon rice wine or sherry
1$^1/_2$-inch piece peeled ginger root, thinly shredded
2 tablespoons sunflower oil

We first invited Deh-Ta, an inspiring Chinese chef, to come to teach at the School in 1984. He adored Ireland, and the flavor of our gray sea mullet. It was almost enough to tempt him to move to Ireland. Gray mullet is closely related to the American striped mullet, which can also be used here.

Wash the fish under the cold tap and dry well, inside and out, with paper towels. Slash both sides of the fish diagonally as far as the bone at $^1/_2$-inch intervals with a sharp knife. Rub half the salt and all the sesame seed oil inside the fish, and place it on top of 2–3 scallions in an oval dish. Mix the mushrooms and pork or ham with the remaining salt, a little of the soy sauce, and the rice wine or sherry. Stuff the fish with half the mixture. Put the rest on top with the ginger. Place in a hot steamer. Steam vigorously for 15 minutes.

Meanwhile, shred the remaining scallions thinly. Heat the sunflower oil in a little saucepan until bubbling. Remove the fish dish from the steamer and arrange the scallion shreds on top. Pour the remaining soy sauce over the fish and then the hot oil, from head to tail. Serve hot.

Baked Trout with Spinach-Butter Sauce

SERVES 4

2 rainbow trout, weighing 2 pounds each
Salt and freshly ground pepper
2-4 tablespoons butter
2 sprigs of fresh herb fennel

SPINACH-BUTTER SAUCE
1 cup spinach leaves
$^2/_3$ cup heavy cream
6 tablespoons butter

We can sometimes get lovely fat pink trout about 2 years old, which have a wonderful taste—much better than the smaller ones. This is a horrendously rich-sounding sauce, but it's delicious and the flavor is sublime.

Preheat the oven to 375°F.

Clean the trout and wash well, making sure to remove the line of blood from the inside near the backbone. Dry with paper towels and season inside and out with salt and freshly ground pepper. Put a lump of butter and a sprig of fennel into the center of each trout. Take a large sheet of aluminum foil and smear a little butter on the center. Put the trout onto the buttered bit and fold over the edges into a papillote shape. Seal well to ensure that none of the juices can escape. Repeat with the other trout. Put the two foil parcels on a baking sheet, making sure they are not touching. Bake in the preheated oven for about 30 minutes.

Meanwhile, make the spinach-butter sauce. Remove any large stems from the spinach and wash well. Cook in $2^1/_2$ cups salted boiling water for 4–5 minutes or until just soft and tender. Drain, pressing out every last drop of water, then mince the spinach. Put the cream into a saucepan and simmer on low heat until reduced to about 3 tablespoons. Then, on very low heat, whisk in the butter bit by bit as though you were making a Hollandaise sauce. Stir in the spinach.

When the fish is cooked, open the parcels and use some of the delicious juices to thin the sauce. Put the two parcels on a hot serving dish and bring to the table. Skin the fish and lift the juicy pink flesh onto hot plates. Spoon the spinach-butter sauce over the fish and eat immediately.

Chicken with Morels

SERVES 4–6

1 free-range chicken, weighing
3¹/₂ pounds
Salt and freshly ground black pepper
2 tablespoons unsalted butter
1¹/₂ cups Chardonnay or Meursault
6 cloves garlic, unpeeled
1 bouquet garni (with a few parsley
stems, a sprig of fresh thyme, a sprig
of fresh tarragon, and a scrap of
bay leaf)
2 ounces dried morels or 4 ounces
trimmed fresh morels
²/₃–1 cup Homemade Chicken Stock
(see page 184)
1 cup heavy cream
A little Roux (see page 182)

GARNISH
Sprigs of fresh flat leaf parsley

Morels start to appear in the woods from about St. Patrick's Day—mid-March onward. People are notoriously secretive about their sources, not surprisingly. When you are choosing fresh morels they should have a very heavy perfume. Use as many as you can find or afford; in this recipe just 2 ounces fresh morels will perfume the sauce deliciously, but 8 ounces would be even better. Dried morels should be kept in a sealed, dry jar. Always buy the best you can afford and try not to buy more than you need.

Preheat the oven to 350°F.

Season the cavity and breast of the chicken with salt and pepper. Smear the butter over the breast and legs. Put into a flameproof casserole with the wine, unpeeled garlic, and bouquet garni. Bring to a boil on top of the stove, then cover and transfer to the preheated oven to cook for 1¹/₄–1¹/₂ hours, depending on the size of the chicken. If the morels are dried, cover with boiling chicken stock and let soak for 1 hour.

As soon as the chicken is cooked (the internal temperature should be at least 170°F), transfer to a carving dish and keep warm. Skim the fat from the pan juices with a metal spoon, and remove the garlic and bouquet garni. Add the cream, bring to a boil, and thicken by reduction, or, better still, whisk in just a little roux. If the morels are fresh, wash them carefully to remove all traces of grit or soil. Melt a little butter in a hot pan, and toss the morels gently for 2–3 minutes. Season with salt and pepper. Add the morels (and their soaking liquid, if using dried ones) to the sauce. Simmer gently for 5 minutes. Meanwhile, carve the chicken and arrange on a serving dish. Taste the sauce and season if necessary. Spoon the sauce over the chicken and divide the morels equally among each helping. Garnish simply with a little flat-leaf parsley and serve immediately.

Easter Lamb with Roasted Scallions

SERVES 6–8

I leg of spring lamb
Salt and freshly ground black pepper
12–18 scallions, trimmed

GRAVY

2½ cups Homemade Lamb or
Chicken Stock (see page 184)
A little Roux (see page 182)
Salt and freshly ground black pepper

Mint Sauce (see page 188)

GARNISH

Sprigs of fresh mint and parsley

Young spring lamb is sweet and succulent and needs absolutely no embellishment, apart from a dusting of salt and pepper and a little fresh Mint Sauce, made from the first tender sprigs of mint from the cold frame in the kitchen garden. I have a standing order with Mr. Cuddigan, from one year to the next, for spring lamb. For me this is the quintessential taste of Easter. The first mint of the year only just appears in our garden in time for Easter, and when the festival is very early it's touch and go as to whether we will have enough for Mint Sauce.

Preheat the oven to 350°F.

If possible, ask your butcher to remove the hip bone from the leg of lamb so that it will be easier to carve later, then trim the shank end of the leg. Season with salt and pepper. Put into a roasting pan and roast in the preheated oven for I–I¼ hours for rare meat (130°F), I¼–I½ hours for medium (140–145°F), and I½–2 hours for well done (160°F), depending on size. Add the scallions for the last 20 minutes or so.

When the lamb is done to your taste, remove it and the scallions to a carving dish. Let the meat rest for 10 minutes before carving.

Meanwhile, make the gravy. Remove the fat from the juices in the roasting pan with a metal spoon, then add the stock. Bring to a boil, and whisk in a little roux to thicken slightly. Let bubble up until the flavor is concentrated enough. Correct the seasoning and serve the gravy with the garnished lamb, mint sauce, scallions, and lots of crusty roast potatoes.

Risotto with Fava Beans, Green Peas, Asparagus, and Sugar Snaps

SERVES 8

2 cups shelled fava beans
Salt and freshly ground black pepper
1 cup sugar snaps
6 asparagus spears
1¹/₂ cups shelled peas
2 quarts Homemade
Chicken Stock (see page 184)
3 tablespoons butter
²/₃ cup minced onion
1³/₄ cups Carnaroli or Arborio rice
6 tablespoons dry white wine
¹/₄ cup freshly grated Parmesan
(Parmigiano Reggiano), plus
extra for serving

I like my risottos to be soft and soupy. Make sure that the vegetables you use for this dish are fresh and have a bright green color. We make this at the end of spring, when the first of the crop are coming up in the vegetable garden and greenhouse.

Bring 2¹/₂ cups water to a boil in a saucepan, add the fava beans and salt, and cook for 2–3 minutes, or until almost tender. Drain and refresh in cold water. Slip the beans out of their skins.

Meanwhile, cook the sugar snaps, again in boiling salted water, until *al dente*, and cook the asparagus for just 4–5 minutes. Cook the peas for 3–4 minutes. If you can keep your eye on several pots at the same time, do all this while cooking the risotto.

To start the risotto, bring the chicken stock to a boil at the back of the stove, and keep at a low simmer. Melt 2 tablespoons of the butter in a large saucepan, add the minced onion, and cook over medium heat until soft but not colored. Add the rice and a generous pinch of salt. Stir the rice over the heat for 2–3 minutes or until it turns translucent, then increase the heat and add the dry white wine.

When the wine has evaporated, add a couple of ladles of stock and stir. Reduce the heat to medium; keep stirring. When the liquid has almost been absorbed, add another ladleful, stirring all the time. After about 10 minutes, add the beans, peas, and sugar snaps. Continue to ladle in more stock as it is absorbed. After about 5 more minutes, taste the rice: it should be just cooked. Stir in the remaining butter, the freshly grated Parmesan, and the asparagus—cut at an angle in 1-inch pieces. Add a little more stock if necessary—the risotto should be moist. Taste and correct the seasoning.

Serve immediately in hot bowls, with extra freshly grated Parmesan as required to sprinkle over the top.

Seakale with Melted Butter

SERVES 4–6

1 pound seakale
4–6 tablespoons butter, melted
Salt and freshly ground black pepper

We grow seakale (Crambe maritima) in the herb garden and in the kitchen garden—it is never found in the market, so it is really worth planting seeds (available by mail order). You will need plastic buckets or, in an ideal world, terracotta seakale pots, to blanch it from November to April. I have lots of blanching pots made by the Whichford Pottery. I was so sorely tempted when I saw them at the Chelsea Flower Show in London, that I went on a mighty spree and had to hide the evidence from Timmy for ages!

Wash the seakale gently and trim into manageable lengths—about 4 inches. Bring about 2½ cups of water to a fast rolling boil and add 1 teaspoon of salt. Pop in the seakale, cover, and boil until tender—5–15 minutes, depending on the thickness.

Just as soon as a knife pierces the seakale easily, drain it. Serve on hot plates with a little melted butter and perhaps a few small triangles of toast. At the beginning of its short season in April, we eat it on hot toast with melted butter or Hollandaise Sauce (see page 182). When the crop becomes more abundant it makes a wonderful accompaniment to fish, particularly wild Irish salmon (see page 30) or sea trout.

Cardoons Layered with Parmesan

SERVES 6

4 pounds cardoons, trimmed
Water acidulated with the juice of a
lemon
Butter
Salt and freshly ground black pepper
Parmesan cheese (Parmigiano Reggiano
is the best), freshly grated
Cream

Cardoons look very like their cousin, the globe artichoke, but are cultivated for their stalks, not their thistle-like flowers. We have been growing them at Ballymaloe for about a decade now.

Preheat the oven to 400°F.

Separate the cardoon stalks from the hearts. Save the tender hearts for eating raw, if you like. Cut the stalks into manageable lengths, say 3–4 inches, and cook in acidulated water for 30–35 minutes. Drain and refresh in cold water; remove the strings from the outer stalks.

Smear a baking dish with butter and arrange a layer of cardoons in the bottom. Dot with butter, season with salt and pepper, and sprinkle with freshly grated Parmesan. Then add another layer of cardoons, butter, more seasoning, and Parmesan. Continue adding layers until the dish is full, finishing with a layer of cardoons. Pour on a little cream and sprinkle the top with Parmesan cheese. Bake in the preheated oven for 15–20 minutes or until the cardoons are tender and the top is bubbling and golden.

Buttered Kale

SERVES 6

3 pounds kale
2 quarts water
1¹/₂ teaspoons salt
2–4 tablespoons butter
Salt and freshly ground black pepper

One of the most treasured plants in our vegetable garden is a very ancient type of perennial kale with many local names. It is sometimes called "cut and come," "cottier's kale," "winter greens," or, most appropriate of all, "hungry gap," which refers to the fact that this humble, everlasting kale is the only green vegetable to cheer and nourish during the barren period between winter and early spring when nothing else is ready to harvest. This type of kale, Brassica oleracea, is thought to be about 2000 years old and is of tremendous interest to botanists.

This kale was unknown to me until a few years ago when I came across it in the eighteenth-century walled garden at Glin Castle in County Limerick. The gardener, Tom Wall, gave me a few slips, which I planted in our vegetable garden. That real treasure has increased and multiplied, and every year from late winter to early spring it produces a wealth of tender greens. True to its local name, the more one cuts the more it comes. It has the flavor of kale, but the melting texture of spinach.

Trim the stems and wash the kale. Bring the water to a fast rolling boil in a saucepan and add the salt and kale. Cook uncovered for about 25 minutes or until tender. Drain off all the water and season well with salt and pepper. Chop the kale well, then beat in a really generous lump of butter. Taste and adjust the seasoning if you need to.

Braised Turnips with Annual Marjoram

SERVES 4–6

I pound small turnips
I–2 tablespoons butter
Salt and freshly ground white pepper
Freshly chopped annual
marjoram or oregano, plus a couple
of sprigs

These turnips are best in the late spring, when they just fit in the palm of the hand. This recipe is sensational on its own, but particularly delicious with duck and lamb. Don't throw away the turnip tops; save them for wilted greens or soup.

Wash and peel the turnips. Quarter or thickly slice the turnips. Melt a lump of butter in a flameproof casserole and toss in the turnip until it is barely coated. Season with salt and pepper. Add no more than a tablespoon of water and a couple of sprigs of annual marjoram or oregano. Cover with a buttered piece of parchment paper and the casserole lid. Cook over low heat for 8–10 minutes or until the turnips are just tender. Remove the sprigs and add a little freshly chopped marjoram. Taste and correct the seasoning, then serve.

Scallion Champ

SERVES 4–6

6–8 potatoes suitable for mashing
$^1/_4$–$^1/_2$ cup finely chopped scallions or
fresh chives
I$^1/_4$–I$^1/_2$ cups milk
4–8 tablespoons butter
Salt and freshly ground black pepper

A bowl of mashed potatoes flecked with green scallions and a lump of butter melting in the center is "comfort" food at its best.

Scrub the potatoes and boil them in their jackets. Cover the scallions or chives with cold milk and bring slowly to a boil. Simmer for about 3–4 minutes, then remove from the heat and let infuse. Peel and mash the potatoes. While hot, mix with the boiling milk and scallions or chives. Beat in half the butter. Season to taste with salt and freshly ground pepper. Serve in a large bowl with the remaining butter melting in the center.

You can reheat the "champ" later in a preheated oven at 350°F. Cover with foil while it reheats to prevent a crust from forming on the top.

Spring Creams with Green Gooseberry and Elderflower Compote

SERVES 6–8

SPRING CREAMS
2¹/₂ cups heavy cream
1–2 vanilla beans, split lengthwise
¹/₄ cup sugar
Scant 2 teaspoons unflavored gelatin
2 tablespoons water

GOOSEBERRY AND ELDERFLOWER
COMPOTE
2 pounds green gooseberries
2–3 elderflower heads
2¹/₄ cups sugar
2¹/₂ cups water

DECORATION
Gooseberry leaves (optional)
Softly whipped cream
Light brown sugar

YOU WILL NEED
6–8 molds (about ¹/₂ cup capacity)
lightly brushed with a non-scented oil
such as sunflower or peanut

In May, the whole of the Irish countryside is full of elder blooms. We used to be nervous of the tree as children, because there is an old Irish saying that if you hit someone with an elder twig they will not grow any taller. But now, as soon as we see the flowers, we rush out to the fruit garden to check the size of the gooseberries. I would love to congratulate the first person who thought of combining these two ingredients. When they cook together the muscatel flavor of the elder blossoms balances the tartness of the gooseberries magically. Eat it on its own, with ice cream, with carrageen-moss pudding, or with these delectable Spring Creams, which are completely exquisite when made with our rich Irish cream.

First make the Spring Creams. Put the cream into a heavy saucepan with the split vanilla beans and sugar. Put on a low heat and bring to the "shivery" stage.

Meanwhile, soften the gelatin in the water. Set the bowl in a saucepan of simmering water until the gelatin has dissolved. Add a little of the cream to the gelatin, then stir both mixtures together. Remove the vanilla beans and then pour into the molds. When cold, cover and refrigerate until set, preferably overnight.

Next, make the compote. Trim the gooseberries. Tie the elderflower heads in a little square of cheesecloth, put in a stainless steel or enameled saucepan, add the sugar, and cover with the water. Bring to a boil slowly and simmer gently for 2 minutes. Add the gooseberries and simmer just until the fruit bursts. Leave to cool, then remove the elderflowers.

To serve: put a large gooseberry leaf on a plate. Unmold a wobbly Spring Cream carefully onto or beside the leaf and spoon a little of the compote onto the plate. Put a blob of softly whipped cream on the side. Sprinkle this with brown sugar and serve immediately.

Semifreddo di Mandorle

SERVES 20–25

PRALINE
$^1/_2$ cup sugar
$^2/_3$ cup unskinned almonds

2 cups heavy cream
$^1/_2$ cup sugar

5 free-range eggs, separated
$^1/_4$ cup sugar

DECORATION
Extra praline: $^1/_2$ cup sugar
and $^1/_2$ cup almonds

YOU WILL NEED
2 loaf pans lined with
plastic wrap

This exquisite dinner-party dessert comes from Erice in Sicily. It is very easy to make, but, as ever, its flavor depends on having really good-quality ingredients. It is also delicious served with bitter chocolate sauce or with fresh raspberries, loganberries, or mulberries in late summer. It is truly superb with the Kumquat Compote (see page 173).

First make the praline. Put the sugar and unskinned almonds into a heavy sauté pan and cook over low heat until the sugar gradually melts and turns to a rich caramel color; do not stir. When the sugar has caramelized, and not before, carefully rotate the pan until the nuts are all covered with caramel. When the nuts go "pop," pour the praline onto a lightly oiled jelly roll pan or oiled marble slab. Let cool completely. When the praline is quite hard, crush in a food processor or with a rolling pin. The texture should be quite coarse and gritty.

Meanwhile, whip the chilled cream with the sugar until softly whipped. Cover and keep in the refrigerator until needed. Whisk the egg yolks with the sugar until light and fluffy, then fold in the whipped cream very delicately. Fold the crushed praline into the mousse. Beat the egg whites stiffly and fold gently, little by little, into the mixture. Divide between the loaf pans. Cover and freeze for a minimum of 3 hours or a maximum of 1 month.

Meanwhile, make some more praline as before, grind coarsely, and set aside.

To serve: cut the semifreddo into slices no more than $^1/_2$ inch thick. Sprinkle a layer of finely crushed praline over each slice. Serve immediately on chilled plates.

February Citrus Fruit Salad

SERVES ABOUT 6

1/2 pound kumquats
1 cup sugar
1 1/2 cups water
1 lime
2–4 tangerines or mandarins
3–4 clementines
1 pink grapefruit
2 blood oranges
Lemon juice to taste, if necessary

In the winter, when many fruits have abysmal flavor, the citrus fruits are at their best. This delicious, fresh-tasting salad uses a wide variety of the ever-expanding citrus family. It's particularly good when a few blood oranges are included. Ugli fruit, pomelo, tangelos, and sweeties all add excitement and zingy flavor. A great palate cleaner after a heavy winter meal.

Slice the kumquats into 1/4-inch rounds and remove the seeds. Dissolve the sugar in the water over low heat and add the sliced kumquats. Cover and simmer for about 30 minutes or until tender. Remove from the heat. Let cool.

Meanwhile, remove the zest from the lime with a citrus zester. Add with its juice to the kumquats. Peel the tangerines or mandarins and clementines and remove as much of the white pith and strings as possible. Cut into rounds of 1/4-inch thickness and add to the syrup. Section the pink grapefruit and blood oranges and add to the syrup, too. Let macerate for at least an hour. Taste and add a squeeze of lemon juice, if necessary.

If the juice is too intense, simply dilute with a little cold water or add some more freshly squeezed blood orange juice to taste. Serve chilled.

Fresh Lemon Ice Cream with Crystallized Lemon Peel

SERVES 4

1 free-range egg, separated
1 cup milk
3/4 cup sugar
1 large lemon

DECORATION
Crystallized lemon peel (see page 189)
Fresh mint leaves and borage flowers

This is a fresh, tangy, light ice cream, easy to make and a delight to eat at the end of any spring meal.

Whisk the egg yolk with the milk. Gradually mix in the sugar. Grate the zest from the lemon carefully on the finest part of a stainless steel grater. Squeeze the juice from the lemon and add with the zest to the liquid. Beat the egg white until quite stiff, and fold into the other ingredients. Freeze in an ice cream machine according to the manufacturer's instructions. Or, put in a covered plastic container and freeze. When the mixture starts to set, remove from the freezer and whisk again, or break up in a food processor. Then put it back in the freezer until it is completely frozen. Meanwhile, chill the serving plates.

To serve: scoop the ice cream into curls and arrange on the chilled plates or in pretty frosted glass dishes. Decorate with crystallized lemon peel, and borage flowers and fresh mint leaves if you have them.

Black-Currant Leaf Sorbet

SERVES ABOUT 6

2 large handfuls of young black-currant
leaves
2¹/₂ cups water
I cup sugar
Freshly squeezed juice of 3 lemons
I egg white (if you do not have an
ice cream machine)

This is a very early spring recipe. I watch excitedly as the little black-currant leaves unfurl on the bush outside the School's dining-room window. The strong taste of the leaves foretells the taste of the summer to come and is so welcome at this time of the year. We also adapt this recipe to make elderflower sorbet. Just replace the black-currant leaves with four or five blooming heads of elderflower.

Crush the black-currant leaves tightly in your hand, then put them into a stainless steel saucepan with the water and sugar. Stir to dissolve the sugar and slowly bring to a boil. Simmer for 2–3 minutes, then set aside to cool completely.* Add the lemon juice and strain. Freeze for 20–25 minutes in an ice cream machine. Serve in chilled glasses or bowls lined with black-currant leaves.

Note: If you do not have an ice cream machine, simply freeze the sorbet in a dish in the freezer; when it is semi-frozen, whisk until smooth and return to the freezer. Whisk again when almost frozen, and fold in the stiffly beaten egg white. Keep in the freezer until required. If you have a food processor, freeze the sorbet completely in a tray, then break it up and work for a few seconds in the processor. Add I slightly beaten egg white, process again, and return to the freezer.

Rhubarb Bread and Butter Pudding

SERVES 6–8

I pound red rhubarb
Sugar

4 tablespoons butter, preferably unsalted
12 slices good-quality white bread, crusts
removed
2 cups cream
I cup milk
4 extra large free-range eggs, beaten
lightly
I teaspoon pure vanilla extract
³/₄ cup plus 2 tablespoons sugar
I tablespoon extra sugar, for sprinkling
on top of the pudding

My brother, Rory O'Connell, introduced me to this fantastic combination, which then fired my imagination, and many experiments have followed. We have been having fun ringing the changes with this recipe. Bread and Butter Pudding is also delicious with apple and cinnamon or even mixed spices. I can't wait to try gooseberry and elder-flower as soon as they come back into season. Don't cut down on the cream in this recipe and don't use too much bread.

Cut the rhubarb into I-inch pieces. Put into a dish and sprinkle with sugar. Let macerate for an hour.

Butter the bread. Arrange four slices, buttered-side down, in one layer in the buttered baking dish. Scatter half the rhubarb over the bread, and cover with another layer of bread, buttered-side down. Scatter the remaining rhubarb on top and cover with the remaining bread, buttered-side down.

Whisk together the cream, milk, eggs, vanilla, and sugar in a bowl. Pour the mixture through a fine strainer over the bread. Sprinkle the extra spoonful

DECORATION
Softly whipped cream

YOU WILL NEED
A deep 8-inch square or round
baking dish
A water bath or roasting pan

of sugar over the top. Let the mixture stand, covered loosely, for at least 1 hour or refrigerate overnight.

Preheat the oven to 350°F.

Bake in a water bath—the water should be boiling and should come halfway up the sides of the baking dish—in the middle of the preheated oven, for about 1 hour or until the top is crisp and golden. Serve the pudding warm, with some softly whipped cream.

Lydia's Almond Cake with Crystallized Violets and Angelica

SERVES 10

CRYSTALLIZED VIOLETS
Sugar
I free-range egg white
Freshly picked, sweet-smelling violets

CAKE
I¹/₃ cups ground almonds
I cup confectioners' sugar
¹/₂ cup plus 2 tablespoons all-purpose
flour
3 free-range egg yolks
¹/₂ cup (I stick) butter, melted

ICING
I¹/₂ cups confectioners' sugar
I¹/₂ tablespoons boiling water

Candied angelica

YOU WILL NEED
A child's clean paintbrush
Parchment paper
A 7-inch layer cake pan

In Lydia Strangman's time, they used to bunch up the violets at Kinoith and send them off to Covent Garden in London. When I first started gardening at Kinoith, I gathered up all the remnants of the violets I could find and made a violet bed. We do not know of a better way to remember Lydia than to crystallize the little flowers to use as precious decoration. Violets appear early in spring and are over by May. The art of crystallizing flowers simply takes patience and a meticulous nature—the sort of job that drives some people around the bend but others adore. If it appeals to you, the work will be well rewarded—the violets look and taste divine. If properly done they will last for months. We store them in a pottery jar or in a tin box interleaved with paper towel. We often make this delicious, rich little cake that keeps well in a tin for ages. A tiny slice is just perfect to nibble slowly with a demi-tasse of espresso or a cup of China tea.

Preheat the oven to 275°F.

First crystallize the violets. The sugar should be absolutely dry, so for extra protection, sift it and dry out on a baking sheet in the preheated oven for about 30 minutes. Break up the egg white slightly with a fork—but it does not need to be fluffy. Using the clean paintbrush, brush the egg white very carefully and sparingly over each petal and into every crevice. Then gently sprinkle some sugar over the violet, coating every part thinly. Place the flower carefully on a parchment-lined baking sheet, and continue with the remaining violets. Let dry overnight in a warm, dry place, such as an airing cupboard, close to a solid fuel stove, or over a radiator.

For the cake, preheat the oven to 350°F. Grease the layer cake pan well with melted butter and dust with a little flour. Put the ground almonds, the

confectioners' sugar, and flour into a bowl and mix thoroughly. Make a well in the center and add the egg yolks and the cooled melted butter. Stir well until all the ingredients are thoroughly mixed. Spread the batter evenly in the prepared pan. Make a little hollow in the center and tap the pan on the work surface to release any large air bubbles.

Bake in the preheated oven for 40–45 minutes. The cake should still be moist but cooked through. Let cool in the pan for 5–6 minutes before unmolding onto a wire rack. Let the cake cool completely.

Sift the confectioners' sugar into a bowl and mix to a thickish, smooth icing with the boiling water. Use a metal spatula, dipped in boiling water then dried, to spread the icing gently over the top and sides of the cake.

Decorate with the crystallized violets and little diamonds of candied angelica.

Black-Currant Leaf
Lemonade

SERVES 6–8

INGREDIENTS AS PAGE 46

3–4 cups still or sparkling water

Make the Black-Currant Leaf Sorbet mixture up to the point marked*, then add 3 cups of the water. Taste and add more water if necessary. Serve chilled, with lots of ice.

Summer

The garden bursts into life. After the lean months of Spring, suddenly there is an abundance of vegetables. It's impossible to use them all up, but at last we're spoiled for choice! Fava beans come first, and then we feast on one vegetable after the other: globe artichokes, baby carrots, and tiny beets are pulled from the rich soil minutes before they're cooked and gobbled up; fresh and bright spinach, masses of arugula, radishes, scallions, and all the good things of the salad bowl. Rampaging is all part of a logical whole as far as I'm concerned; we grow the stuff, we cook with it, and the waste goes back to the hens, the compost, the pigs, and so on.

The salad bowl is an integral part of lunch at the Cookery School. Up to forty-four students come ravenously to the dining room, eager to taste the fruits of their labors during the morning. We use tiny ruby chard, carrot tops, and mustard greens. Flowers, too, go into the tapestry—colorful chives, sage, nasturtiums, and zucchini blossoms, and when we've plenty of these last we stuff them with local goat cheese or tomato fondue.

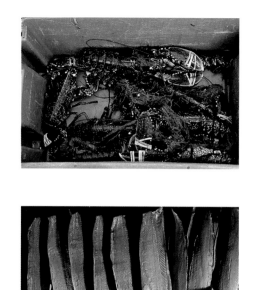

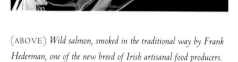

(ABOVE) *Wild salmon, smoked in the traditional way by Frank Hederman, one of the new breed of Irish artisanal food producers.*

(RIGHT) *Choosing fresh lobsters for the School at Ballycotton.*

(FAR RIGHT) *Looking out through the sound at Ballycotton. Our local fishermen are hardworking and adventurous, and we feast gratefully on their catches.*

The first of the smoked eel, warm from the smokehouse, signifies the start of summer. We feast on it, with a bit of lemon, soda bread, and some of the very first vine-ripened tomatoes, grateful that Mrs. Schwartau from Barnabrow had telephoned to tell us the eel was ready. Once the weather settles, out go the lobster pots. We have shrimp, crabs, summer plaice, and lemon sole, which are sweet and tender and melting. The fishermen bring them into Ballycotton, the little fishing village on the coast two miles from us. Every Friday, Dot Haynes drives over from Kilmacalogue Harbour on the Beara peninsula with whatever shellfish are in season, and we get scallops, clams, and sea urchins. Sometimes she brings periwinkles and roghans (blue octopus), and from July onward, she brings chanterelles and whatever other wild mushrooms she can find. Frank Hederman is the man from Belvelly who brings us mussels, salmon, and eel, smoked in the old traditional ways. Bill Casey also smokes wonderful salmon on our farm. The quality of fish we're offered is fantastic.

(ABOVE) *Elizabeth O'Connell, my sister, is head gardener at Kinoith. She, Haulie and Eileen, front up the ace team which nurtures all our wonderfully abundant fresh produce.*

(LEFT) *Sunflowers* (Helianthus annuus) *last incredibly well in flower arrangements. We harvest their edible seeds, to toast, nibble and add to winter salads.*

(RIGHT) *We are forever trying out new herbs, such as this one, ginger mint* (Mentha sauveolents "Variegta"), *which makes a gorgeous flavoring for ice cream.*

If we're lucky, new potatoes from the greenhouse coincide with the first salmon catch of the year, and the herb garden comes to a climax. It is based on a formal parterre, with little box hedges around each of the beds. We grow over 70 different herbs. We use the fresh green leaves and flowers, and later we dry some of the seeds like coriander, fennel, and dill for spices. Fresh coriander (or cilantro) goes into the Thai dishes we're experimenting with and into the salsas, which we all adore since our trip to Mexico.

The fruit garden is just outside the School's dining room. My friend Jim Reynolds, a great garden designer and plantsman, created the design for me and now it provides us with a fantastic crop of berries—loganberries, boysenberries, Worcesterberries, yellow raspberries, and the first strawberries, which Timmy crushes to make muesli for us girls, Lydia, Emily, and me: he soaks fine oats in water and sweetens them with some of our own honey, then serves this for breakfast with rich cream and brown sugar. Delicious!

The Irish Peach tree on the wall has seven apples. It's an old apple variety I've rescued, so named because the fruit tastes of peaches. The almond tree is covered with soft, furry fruits for the first time. When Madhur Jaffrey was here, she told

(RIGHT) *The beach hedges at Kinoith give tremendous shelter and also form marvelous architectural features, dividing up the gardens and affording surprise views through their "doorways."*

(BELOW) *The herringbone paths of the vegetable garden form a diamond and are bisected by a cross. The bricks came from a local salvage yard.*

(FAR RIGHT) *We grow many flowers at the School for flavor and pleasure. Lilies and nasturtiums, the flowers of which decorate many fresh green salads beautifully. We also cultivate marguerites and petunias for summer color.*

us we could eat them whole when they're green. We've put the blueberries and cranberries in peat pots, as they don't like our limey soil. It's difficult to believe that this garden is just five years old. The growth is truly amazing, and the soil rich and fertile from all the farmyard manure, compost, and seaweed that has been dug in. Our neighbors, the Walshes, three generations of them, have been growing more and more fruit—producing wonderful crops of tayberries, loganberries, boysenberries, raspberries, and strawberries—to make into jams and jellies, which we sell at the School. And Patty Walsh rears pigs, too.

The barbecue course in midsummer is the best fun. We teach the students about marinating and kebab-making, stretching their imaginations. We grill kidneys, fresh mackerel from the sea, and butterflied legs of lamb as well as lots of vegetables. When I travel, I eat in new restaurants and buy lots of cookbooks, and that inspires me to try new dishes. Sometimes the recipe is exquisite exactly as it is, and sometimes I wonder what it would taste like if I added this or that to it. I write a few notes and try it. Not everybody's cookbooks delight me. Some I buy just for ideas, but in others I follow every word of genius, like an apostle!

This year's garden development has been to plant the yew tree maze, which covers almost an acre. It was a nightmare to mark out—it couldn't be even a quarter of an inch out in the planting or it would look dreadful. It took ten days to plant; the design is based on an old Celtic pattern and was drawn out by my friend Peter Lamb. Lesley Beck reworked the design to ensure a strong puzzle and to provide a short exit. In ten to fifteen years' time it should have matured. Who'll trim the hedges? I've wanted to plant a maze since the Year of the Maze in 1992, and had the sudden brainwave of planting it as a present for Timmy. Amazingly, he was not immediately thrilled by my gallant gesture, possibly suspecting that he might have to pay for it in the end. However, he came around, and now that it's finally planted, we're both thrilled with it. It's such a bit of nonsense and fantastically flamboyant and almost irresponsible. When I think of the money that has gone into it! But then I don't want a yacht in the Caribbean or anything like that. I prefer to put the money into creating gardens for all of us to enjoy throughout the seasons.

Spinach and Rosemary Soup

SERVES 6–8

4 tablespoons butter
$^3/_4$ cup chopped onion
I cup chopped potatoes
Salt and freshly ground black pepper
$2^1/_2$ cups Homemade Chicken Stock
(see page 184), Vegetable Stock
(see page 185) or water
$1^3/_4$–$2^1/_2$ cups half-and-half
4–6 cups chopped spinach,
stems removed
I tablespoon chopped fresh rosemary

GARNISH
2 heaping tablespoons whipped cream
(optional)
Sprigs of fresh rosemary

We have spinach all year round. You can use either perpetual or summer spinach. The trick with these green soups is not to add the greens until the last minute, otherwise they will overcook and you will lose the fresh taste and bright lively color.

Melt the butter in a heavy-bottomed saucepan. When it foams, add the onions and potatoes and turn them until well coated. Sprinkle with salt and pepper. Cover and sweat on a gentle heat for 10 minutes. Add the boiling stock and milk, bring back to a boil, and simmer until the potatoes and onions are fully cooked. Add the spinach and boil with the lid off for about 3–5 minutes, until the spinach is tender. Add the chopped rosemary. Purée in a blender, then taste. Serve in warm bowls garnished with a blob of whipped cream and a sprig of rosemary.

Pea and Cilantro Soup

SERVES ABOUT 6

4 tablespoons butter
I cup minced onion
2 cloves garlic, minced
I hot green chile pepper, seeded and
minced
3 cups shelled fresh peas (good-quality
frozen ones are also fine)
4 cups Homemade Chicken
Stock (see page 184)
About 2 tablespoons chopped fresh
cilantro
Salt and freshly ground black pepper
Sugar

GARNISH
Soflty whipped cream
Fresh cilantro leaves

This utterly delicious soup has a perky zing with the addition of fresh chile.

Melt the butter over low heat and sweat the onion, garlic, and chile for 3–4 minutes. Add the peas and cover with the stock. Bring to a boil and simmer for 7–8 minutes. Add the freshly chopped cilantro. Purée in a blender or food processor, then reheat, if necessary. Season with salt and pepper, and add a pinch of sugar, which enhances the flavor. Serve with a swirl of softly whipped cream and a few fresh cilantro leaves.

Light Fish Soup with Scallions

SERVES 6

$^1/_2$ pound sole or flounder fillets, skinned
5 cups very well-flavored Basic Chinese
Stock (see page 185)
Salt and lots of freshly ground white pepper
$^1/_2$–I hot red or green chile pepper, thinly sliced
18 large shrimp or 30 medium
shrimp, cooked and peeled
I iceberg lettuce heart, about
I cup very finely shredded

GARNISH

2 tablespoons scallions, finely sliced at an angle
Shrimp roe (eggs), if available
Fresh cilantro or flat-leaf parsley

We adore these light fish soups. Consider this recipe as a formula, and vary the fish and shellfish depending on what you have available—mussels and white crab meat are particularly delicious. We get Atlantic shrimp; if you are using the larger Pacific shrimp, you need fewer. Lemon grass and a dice of cucumber also work well.

Cut the fish fillets at an angle into pieces about 2 inches wide. When you are ready to eat, bring the stock to a boil and add the salt, chile, and pieces of fish. Simmer for I minute. Add the shrimp and heat through.

Put 2 heaping tablespoons of the shredded lettuce into each soup bowl and season generously with pepper. Immediately ladle the boiling soup over it. Garnish with scallions, shrimp roe, and lots of cilantro or parsley. Serve very hot.

Vine-Ripened Tomato and Spearmint Soup

SERVES 6

²/₃ cup minced onion
I tablespoon butter
3 cups Vine-Ripened Tomato
Purée (see page 182)
I cup Béchamel Sauce (see page 182)
I cup Homemade Chicken Stock
(see page 184) or Vegetable Stock
About 2 tablespoons chopped fresh
spearmint
Salt and freshly ground black pepper
Sugar

GARNISH

Whipped cream, with freshly chopped
spearmint leaves added

In late August, we have a glut of intensely flavored tomatoes and basil, which could also be used for this recipe. It is quite tricky to balance this soup—avoid making it too strong or too thick by diluting it with stock. It needs to be tasted carefully, as the final result depends on the quality of the ingredients.

Sweat the onion in the butter on low heat until soft but not colored. Add the tomato purée, béchamel sauce, and chicken or vegetable stock. Add the chopped spearmint and season with salt, pepper, and a large pinch of sugar. Bring to a boil and simmer for a few minutes.

Purée in a blender or food processor, then taste and dilute further with stock if necessary. Bring back to a boil, correct the seasoning, and serve with a swirl of mint-flavored cream.

Ballycotton Shrimp with Chile, Cilantro, and Lemon Grass

SERVES 8

CHILE AND CILANTRO DRESSING
$^1/_2$ fresh hot red chile pepper
$^1/_2$ stem lemon grass
2 tablespoons coarsely chopped
fresh cilantro
$2^1/_2$ tablespoons nam pla (fish sauce)
3 tablespoons freshly squeezed
lemon juice
2 teaspoons light brown sugar
$2^1/_2$ tablespoons dry white wine
I pound fresh shrimp or Dublin Bay
prawns (langoustines), peeled and
cooked

GARNISH
Sprigs of fresh cilantro

Many people are surprised to find lemon grass growing in Shanagarry, but we have been growing it successfully in the greenhouse for the past year or so, and have at last managed to divide and repot the original precious plants. At first I tended to use it sparingly, but now, as it becomes ever more abundant, I have relaxed and use it lavishly to give many of our local foods a fresh and tangy Thai flavor. It works superbly with shrimp caught in Ballycotton Bay.

First make the dressing. Roll the chile on a board to loosen the seeds, and slice off the top. Taste a little—chiles vary a lot in degree of heat, as you know! Shake out the seeds and mince the flesh. Peel the outer leaves from the lemon grass, then mince. Mix with the chile, chopped cilantro, fish sauce, freshly squeezed lemon juice, sugar, and white wine in a bowl. Put the shrimp or prawns into the dressing, cover, and let marinate in the refrigerator for I–2 hours.

Serve the shellfish with some of the dressing spooned over the top. Garnish with sprigs of fresh cilantro and serve with crusty bread.

Quesadillas with Squash Blossoms, Mozzarella, Guacamole, and Tomato Salsa

SERVES 2–4

4–16 squash blossoms,
depending on size
4 corn or wheat flour tortillas
$^1/_2$ pound mozzarella, grated (unless
Oaxacan string cheese is available)
2 hot green chile peppers (optional)

GARNISH
Fresh cilantro

ACCOMPANIMENTS
Guacamole (see page 187)
Tomato and Cilantro Salsa
(see page 187)

Quesadillas are one of the favorite snacks in Mexico. On Sundays, in Oaxaca, women make and sell these and many other delicious stuffed tortillas on little stalls in the streets and squares. A favorite filling for quesadillas in Oaxaca is simply grated Oaxacan string cheese (mozzarella is our nearest equivalent) and fresh squash blossoms.

First make the Guacamole and Tomato and Cilantro Salsa. Cover and keep cool. Remove the thorns from the base of the squash blossoms. Heat a cast-iron skillet or griddle; it should be medium hot, otherwise the outside of the tortillas will burn before the filling is cooked.

There are two ways of presenting quesadillas: one resembles a sandwich, the other a turnover. Lay a tortilla on the hot skillet and put about 2 tablespoons of cheese on the tortilla, keeping it a little from the edge. Sprinkle some strips or dice of chile on top with I–4 squash blossoms and another 2 tablespoons of cheese. Fold the tortilla over the filling and cook for a minute or two, then turn it over carefully. Cook just until the cheese begins to melt. Serve one or two per person with the Guacamole and the Tomato and Cilantro Salsa.

Radishes with Butter, Crusty Bread, and Sea Salt

Fresh radishes complete with leaves
Finest unsalted butter
Sea salt (we use Maldon flakes)

Crusty bread

When I was just nineteen, an au pair in Besançon, alone and frightened, a French girl took pity on me and invited me to have lunch with her in a café. We had a plate of charcuterie and radishes. I watched in fascination as she smeared a little unsalted butter on her radishes, dipped them in sea salt, and ate them greedily. I followed suit—and I've never forgotten the flavor. We use Bill Hogan's fine unsalted butter churned from morning cream whenever we can get it.

Wash the radishes and trim the root, and the top of the leaves if they are long.

Cut a chunk of butter into 1/2-inch cubes. If you have a pair of butter pats, soak them in cold water and then use to roll each cube into a ball; drop into a bowl of ice water.

To serve: put 7 or 8 chilled radishes on each plate and add 2 or 3 butter balls and a little mound of sea salt.

Serve fresh crusty bread as an accompaniment.

Stuffed Zucchini Blossoms with Goat Cheese, Pesto, and Tomato Fondue

SERVES 6–8

BATTER

1 cup all-purpose flour
1¹/₂ tablespoons olive oil
1–1¹/₂ free-range egg whites
Sea salt

Sunflower oil for deep-frying
12–16 male zucchini flowers

FILLING

6–8 ounces fresh goat cheese (I use
St. Tola, Croghan, or Ardsallagh, each
wonderful but different)
3–4 teaspoons Pesto (see page 186)
3–4 tablespoons Tomato Fondue
(see page 182)

ACCOMPANIMENT

Tomato sauce or extra Tomato Fondue

In the summer we grow zucchini in both the kitchen garden and the greenhouses. They produce hundreds of canary-yellow blossoms. The female flowers produce the fruit, but we use the male flowers in our salads, as a container for sauces, and in soups. They are also utterly delicious stuffed with a few melting morsels, then dipped in a light batter and deep-fried until crisp and golden. This may sound a difficult recipe, but it actually takes seconds. I only suggest this stuffing; let your imagination run riot. Any filling you choose should be juicy and melting.

First make the batter. Sift the flour into a bowl and make a well in the center. Pour in the olive oil, stir, and add enough water to make a batter about the consistency of thick cream. Let stand for at least 1 hour if you can. Just before cooking, beat the egg whites to a stiff peak and fold into the batter. Add salt to taste.

Heat the oil in a deep-fryer until very hot. Remove the thorns from the base of the zucchini flowers and the stamens from the center. Hold a flower upright and open it slightly and carefully. Put about ¹/₂ ounce goat cheese, ¹/₂ teaspoon Pesto, and 1 teaspoon Tomato Fondue into each. Twist the tips of the petals to seal. Dip in the batter and drop into the hot oil. Fry on one side for about 2 minutes and then turn over. They will take about 4 minutes in total to become crisp and golden. You may need to work in batches.

Drain on paper towels and serve immediately—just as they are, or with hot tomato sauce or a little extra Tomato Fondue.

Chargrilled Summer Vegetables with Tapenade Toasts

SERVES 8 (OR 4 AS A MAIN COURSE)

4 medium-sized green (or a mixture of green and golden) zucchini, cut lengthwise in slices $^1/_8$ inch thick
2–3 eggplants, cut in slices $^1/_4$ inch thick
Coarse sea salt
2–3 fleshy red sweet peppers, Italian or Spanish if possible
2–3 fleshy yellow peppers, Italian or Spanish if possible
4–8 asparagus spears
1 Florence fennel bulb, cut lengthwise in slices $^1/_8$ inch thick
Salt and freshly ground black pepper
Extra virgin olive oil

DRESSING

$^1/_3$ cup very best Italian extra virgin olive oil
Freshly squeezed juice of $^1/_4$ lemon or 2 tablespoons balsamic vinegar
Sea salt and freshly crushed black pepper (we crush ours in a mortar and pestle)
10–12 fresh basil leaves (annual marjoram is also very good)
Black olives
Tapenade Toasts (see page 186)
Whole Roasted Garlic (see page 83)

In July, we feast on these chargrilled vegetables as a first course. We use many different combinations, depending on what we have an abundance of. They are also marvelous with goat cheese, with pasta, and with Pesto.

Sprinkle the zucchini and eggplant with sea salt and let drain in a colander to get rid of the excess liquid—30 minutes at least. However, if the zucchini are small, home-grown, and very fresh, this step is not necessary.

Grill the peppers, turning them so they become completely charred on all sides. We do this in various ways: over charcoal, in a gas flame, under the broiler, or in the oven. Remove from the heat and place in a bowl. Cover and leave for 5–10 minutes, to make them easier to peel.

Blanch the asparagus in boiling salted water for no more than 30 seconds, then plunge into ice water to refresh. Drain.

Lay out the zucchini and eggplant slices on paper towels to dry off all the excess liquid. Brush each piece sparingly with olive oil. Grill the eggplant first, over charcoal or on a hot grill pan—they should be soft when pressed and scorched by the grill but not blackened. Put each vegetable onto a large plate as it is cooked. Next grill the zucchini and fennel slices—just give them a few seconds to brown in the places where they touch the grill. Finally, season the blanched asparagus spears with salt and pepper and grill for about $^1/_2$ minute on each side.

The peppers should now be cool. Peel off the charred skin and remove the stem and seeds with your hands. Divide the peppers into four and add to the grilled vegetables. Don't rinse them or you will lose some of their sweet flavor.

For the dressing, mix the extra virgin olive oil with freshly squeezed lemon juice or balsamic vinegar.

Spoon the whisked dressing over the vegetables and toss gently. Taste and season with sea salt and freshly crushed black pepper. Arrange on a large platter. Scatter with basil leaves, a few black olives, freshly cracked pepper, and some sea salt.

Serve with Tapenade Toasts or bruschetta and a few roasted garlic bulbs.

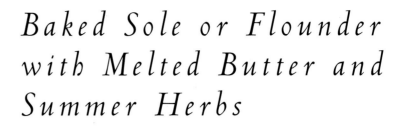

Baked Sole or Flounder with Melted Butter and Summer Herbs

SERVES 4

4 very fresh sole or flounder on the bone
Salt and freshly ground black pepper

HERB BUTTER
$^1/_2$ cup (I stick) butter
4 teaspoons minced mixed fresh parsley,
chives, herb fennel, and thyme

This delectable way of cooking fresh flatfish was the brainchild of my mother-in-law, Myrtle Allen. It can be used not only for flounder and sole, but for all very fresh flatfish, such as turbot and dab. Depending on the size of the fish, it can be a first course or a main course. Because the fish is cooked on the bone, with the skin on, it is particularly sweet and moist, and may be eaten without a sauce. Alternatively, it can be served not only with herb butter but with any other complementary sauce, such as Hollandaise, Beurre Blanc, or Lobster.

Preheat the oven to 350°F.

Lay the fish flat on its side and remove the head. Wash the fish and clean the slits very thoroughly. With a sharp knife, cut through the skin right around the edge of each fish, just where the "fringe" meets the flesh. Be careful to cut neatly and to cross the side cuts at the tail, or it will be difficult to remove the skin later on. Sprinkle the fish with salt and pepper and lay them in $^1/_4$ inch of water in a shallow baking pan.

Bake in the preheated oven for 20–30 minutes, according to the size of the fish. The water should have just evaporated as the fish is cooked. Check to see whether the fish is cooked by lifting the flesh from the bone at the head; it should lift off the bone easily and be quite white with no trace of pink.

Meanwhile, melt the butter, take off the heat, and stir in the freshly minced herbs. Just before serving, catch the skin down near the tail and pull it off gently (the skin will tear badly if not properly cut). Lift the fish onto hot plates and spoon the herb butter over them. Serve immediately, with the remainder of the herb butter in a warm bowl.

To eat: first eat the flesh off the flat frame on top; then put your fork on top, slide your knife underneath the bone, and flip it over gently onto your plate. Lift back the underneath skin with your knife and continue to feast on the sweet flesh. Spoon a little more herb butter over, if desired.

Fresh Eel with Butter and Lemon

SERVES 4–6

2 pounds eel, skinned
All-purpose flour seasoned with salt
and pepper
2 tablespoons butter
I lemon

GARNISH
Segments of lemon
Chopped parsley (optional)

As fresh fish is landed almost daily at Ballycotton, we are unquestionably spoiled for choice. Yet if I were to be completely honest, my favorite fish of all is eel, a freshwater species. We so rarely get them—two or three times a year if we are lucky. I love them prepared in the simplest way, just tossed in seasoned flour and cooked in butter. I have never had any desire to tart them up further. The fish will be so sweet and juicy that you will want to suck the bones—unthinkable but true!

Cut the eel into 3- to 4-inch pieces and toss in seasoned flour.
Melt the butter in a large wide skillet. Cook the pieces of eel over medium heat, first on one side, then on the other, until just cooked through and golden. Transfer the fish to a serving dish or hot plates. Squeeze a little lemon juice into the butter in the skillet, add a little more fresh butter if necessary, and spoon the bubbling liquid over the fish. Serve immediately, with a sprinkling of chopped parsley and some lemon segments.

Madhur Jaffrey's Butterflied Leg of Lamb

SERVES 10–12

1 medium onion, coarsely chopped
Piece of fresh ginger, 3 inches long, 1 inch wide, peeled and coarsely chopped
7 cloves garlic, coarsely chopped
$3/4$ cup freshly squeezed lemon juice
1 tablespoon ground coriander
1 tablespoon ground cumin
1 teaspoon Garam Masala (see below)
1 teaspoon ground turmeric
$1/4$ teaspoon ground mace
$1/4$ teaspoon ground nutmeg
$1/4$ teaspoon ground cinnamon
$1/4$ teaspoon ground cloves
1 cup olive oil
$2–2^1/2$ teaspoons salt
$1/4$ teaspoon freshly ground black pepper

1 leg of lamb, weighing 8-9 pounds, butterflied

GARNISH
Scallions, radishes, and fresh flat-leaf parsley

Madhur has been a guest chef at the School on several occasions. Her classes are always oversubscribed. The students sit spellbound for hours because she is an inspiring lecturer. She has introduced us to many great culinary combinations, some of which have been incorporated into the Ballmaloe repertoire. This recipe, like her spicy kebabs marinated in the same spice blend, is the perfect barbecue dish, a favorite on our summer barbecue course.

Work the onion, ginger, garlic, and 4 tablespoons of lemon juice in a food processor or blender for about a minute. Put this paste into a bowl, add the remaining ingredients, except the meat, and mix well.

Cut off all the fat and sinews from the meat and make lots of holes in it with the point of a knife. Rub the paste well into the meat, making sure it goes into the holes. Cover and refrigerate for 24 hours (or, better still, 48 hours). Turn it over several times during that period.

Prepare a charcoal fire. Lift the meat out of the marinade and drain for a few minutes. Sear on both sides first, then raise the rack to the uppermost notch and cook for 20 minutes on each side. Brush frequently with the marinade until it is all used up. The meat needs to cook for about 50 minutes in total and should be dark on the outside but still pinkish inside. (A meat thermometer should register an internal temperature of 140-145°F for medium.)

To serve: carve the lamb into thin slices with a sharp knife and serve immediately on a hot serving dish, garnished with scallions, radishes, and flat-leaf parsley.

Madhur Jaffrey's Garam Masala

MAKES ABOUT 3 TABLESPOONS

1 tablespoon green cardamom seeds (from the pods)
1-inch piece of cinnamon stick
1 teaspoon cumin seeds
1 teaspoon whole cloves
1 teaspoon black peppercorns
$1/4$ whole nutmeg

Commercial garam masala loses its aromatic flavor very quickly, so it is best to make your own. Grind it in small quantities so that it is always fresh and used up quickly. Don't forget to clean out the coffee grinder really well or your coffee will certainly perk you up! Better still, if you use spices regularly, keep a grinder specially for that purpose.

Put all the ingredients into a clean electric coffee grinder and grind for about 30 seconds or until all the spices are finely ground. Store in a jar with a tight-fitting lid, in a dark place, and use up quickly.

Baby Beef Scaloppine and Spinach with Raisins and Pine Nuts

SERVES 6

1¹/2 pounds lean baby beef from the top round

Salt and freshly ground black pepper

All-purpose flour

Beaten free-range egg

Fresh white bread crumbs

5–6 tablespoons clarified butter

Lemon segments

Spinach with Raisins and Pine Nuts (see page 82)

We do not serve intensively reared veal either at Ballymaloe House or at the Cookery School, but once or twice a year we have a naturally reared milk-fed calf from Sibylle Knobel or one of my own Kerry bull calves. The meat is not as pale as conventional veal, but it is wonderfully sweet and delicious. This is one of Tim's favorite meals, reminding him of the Jersey baby beef of his childhood when his father was a Jersey breeder.

With a very sharp knife, cut the top round into ¹/₄ inch thick slices across the grain. Trim off any fat or sinews. Put between two sheets of plastic wrap and flatten a little more with a meat pounder or rolling pin. Dip each piece in flour, well seasoned with salt and pepper, then in beaten egg and soft white bread crumbs. Pat off the excess.

Heat the clarified butter in a large wide skillet. Fry the scaloppine, a few at a time, until crisp and golden on one side, then flip over onto the other side and fry until golden. Drain briefly on paper towels. Serve hot with segments of lemon and Spinach with Raisins and Pine Nuts.

Frittata with Oven-Roasted Tomatoes and Summer Herbs

SERVES 2–4

I pound cherry tomatoes
Salt and freshly ground black pepper
8 extra large eggs, preferably free-range
I tablespoon chopped parsley
2 teaspoons chopped fresh thyme
I tablespoon chopped fresh basil
or marjoram
I cup freshly grated Gruyère cheese,
1/4 cup freshly grated Parmesan cheese
2 tablespoons butter

Italian frittata, Middle-Eastern kuku, and Spanish tortilla all sound more exciting than a flat omelette, although that is basically what they all are. Unlike their soft and creamy French cousin, these omelettes are cooked slowly over very low heat—while you can be whipping up a delicious salad accompaniment! A frittata is cooked gently on both sides and served in wedges like a cake. Omit the tomato and you have the basic recipe, flavored with cheese and a generous sprinkling of herbs. As with a rolled omelette, you will want to add some tasty morsels to vary the flavor—perhaps some spinach, chard, broccoli, asparagus, or smoked mackerel. The list is endless.

Preheat the oven to 350°F.

Halve the tomatoes around the equator, and season with salt and a little pepper. Arrange in a single layer in a nonstick roasting pan. Roast for 10–15 minutes, or until almost soft and slightly crinkly. Let cool.

Preheat the broiler.

Whisk the eggs in a bowl. Add the herbs, tomatoes, grated cheese, and a seasoning of salt and pepper. Melt the butter in a nonstick skillet that measures 7 1/2 inches across the base and 9 inches across the top. When the butter starts to foam, tip in the egg mixture. Lower the heat to its minimum. Slip a flame tamer under the skillet, then let the frittata cook gently for 15 minutes or until the underside is set. The top should still be slightly runny. Slide the skillet under the preheated broiler, about 4 inches from the heat, and cook for I minute to set and barely brown the surface.

Slip a metal spatula under the frittata to free it from the skillet. Slide onto a warm plate and serve cut in wedges, with a green salad and a few olives.

Pasta with Chanterelles, Tapenade, and Flat-Leaf Parsley

SERVES 4–6

1 tablespoon salt
1/2 pound penne, conchiglie, or farfalle
1/2-1 pound fresh chanterelles
2 tablespoons butter
Salt and freshly ground black pepper
1/2 cup heavy cream
2–3 tablespoons Tapenade (see page 186)

GARNISH
2 tablespoons chopped fresh flat-leaf parsley

Dot Haynes, who delivers shellfish to the School, also brings chanterelles up to us from the Beara peninsula when they are in season (from late July to October).

Bring a very large pot of water to a fast rolling boil, then add the salt and the pasta. Stir well, then cook until *al dente.*

Meanwhile, quickly but gently wash the chanterelles under cold running water. Trim the base of the stems and discard. Slice the mushrooms thickly. Melt the butter in a skillet on high heat. When it foams, add the mushrooms. Season with salt and pepper. Cook on high heat, letting the juices exude at first, then cook until the chanterelles reabsorb them. Add the cream and bubble for a minute or two. Stir in the Tapenade.

Drain the pasta and put back into the pot. Add the sauce. Sprinkle on the parsley, toss gently, turn into a hot bowl, and serve immediately.

Summer Pasta with Zucchini and Sugar Snaps

SERVES 10

I pound green and golden zucchini,
5-6 inches long
I pound sugar snap peas
Salt and freshly ground black pepper
I pound penne or spaghetti
4 tablespoons butter
4 tablespoons olive oil
2 tablespoons chopped parsley
$1^{1}/_{4}$ cups chopped fresh basil leaves
$1^{1}/_{2}$ cups freshly grated Parmesan
cheese (Parmigiano Reggiano is best)

GARNISH
A few zucchini flowers, if available
Fresh basil leaves

Simple, yet—if the Parmesan is good and all the ingredients are fresh—a sublime dish.

Trim the zucchini and cut at an angle into $^{1}/_{4}$-inch slices. String the sugar snaps, if necessary. Bring 6 quarts of water to a boil in a large deep pot and add 2 tablespoons salt. Add the pasta and cook until *al dente*. Meanwhile, shoot the sugar snaps into I quart of boiling water with $1^{1}/_{2}$ teaspoons of salt and cook, uncovered, for 3–4 minutes or until crisp-tender; drain. Put a serving bowl for the pasta into the oven to warm, or, better still, sit it on top of the pasta pot.

If you are adept at juggling and have enough stove space, you can fry the zucchini while the pasta and sugar snaps are cooking. Heat the butter and olive oil in a sauté pan, add the zucchini, and toss for 3–4 minutes. Season with salt and pepper, then cover the pan, and reduce the heat to medium. Cook for a few more minutes, by which time the zucchini should be tender but still firm. Draw off the heat.

By now, if your timing is good, the pasta too should be *al dente*, so drain it quickly. Add the sugar snaps, parsley, and basil to the zucchini. Pour in the steaming hot pasta, sprinkle on two-thirds of the freshly grated Parmesan, and toss well. Taste and adjust the seasoning if necessary.

Turn into the hot serving bowl and garnish with a few zucchini flowers, if available, and basil leaves. Rush to the table, and serve on hot plates with the remaining Parmesan and freshly ground pepper.

Aigre-Doux Onions with Thyme Leaves

SERVES 4–6

1 pound boiling onions
2 tablespoons butter
2 teaspoons fresh thyme leaves
2 tablespoons sugar
2 tablespoons white wine vinegar
Salt and freshly ground black pepper

A basket of baby onions is a real treasure to have in the pantry: we save the small onions of the crop carefully—gorgeous for roasting, sweet and melting, cooked whole in stews or in onion Tartes Tatins, and irresistible with a shiny sweet-sour glaze. Of course you can eat this dish all year round.

Peel and trim the onions, leaving the root base intact. Melt the butter in a heavy saucepan and toss the onions in it. Add the thyme leaves. Cover with buttered parchment paper and a tight-fitting lid. Cook on low heat until almost soft.

Add the sugar and vinegar. Increase the heat and cook until the sugar, vinegar, and onion juices make a syrupy glaze. Season, then spoon into a hot serving dish and serve immediately.

Baby Fava Beans with Olive Oil and Orla Sheep's Milk Cheese

SERVES 6

1 pound shelled baby fava beans—
about 4 pounds in the pods
Extra virgin olive oil
Sea salt
Orla sheep's cheese, Knockalara,
or pecorino romano
Crusty white bread or ciabatta

As my "garden angels," Eileen, Elizabeth, and Haulie, know, fava beans, considered dull by many, are my favorite vegetable. I insist on planting the first seeds in November, so that with luck we will have the first tender beans in early June. With careful successive planting, we manage to have them until the end of October. I use the tangy-tasting, prize-winning sheep's cheese made by Ollie Jungwirth and Iris Diebrok from Manch Farm near Ballineen in West Cork because it is the perfect foil for fava beans—as is Knockalara sheep's milk cheese. Pecorino would be eaten in Italy. You could also use feta or anything slightly crumbly and sharp.

Bring the fresh raw beans to the table, with a bottle of your best extra virgin olive oil, a bowl of sea salt, and a piece of sharpish cheese. Let each person have the pleasure of removing the beans from the furry pods. When you have accumulated a little pile on your plate, dip them, one by one, first into olive oil, then into sea salt. Enjoy with the tangy cheese and warm crusty bread or ciabatta. Thin slices of prosciutto or very good Italian salami would make this a more substantial feast.

Okra in Batter

SERVES 4

¹/₂ pound fresh okra
³/₄ cup all-purpose flour
I¹/₂ tablespoons ground rice or rice flour
I tablespoon cayenne pepper
¹/₂ teaspoon ground cumin
¹/₂ teaspoon ground turmeric
I teaspoon salt
I teaspoon fresh thyme leaves
Olive oil for deep-frying

Among other exotics, we grow okra in the greenhouses. Gumbos are quite a performance, delicious though they are, so try this simple recipe, to serve with fish or meat. We love to eat them with fishcakes.

Slice the caps off the okra and discard them. Cut the stalks into ¹/₂ inch thick rounds.

Sift the all-purpose flour, the ground rice or rice flour, cayenne pepper, cumin, turmeric, and salt into a bowl. Add the thyme leaves, mix well, and make a well in the center. Add about ¹/₂ cup water, whisking it in a little at a time, to make a light batter with the consistency of thick cream.

Heat the oil in a deep-fryer over medium-low heat. Fold the slices of okra gently into the batter and drop tablespoonfuls into the oil carefully. Fry, turning now and then, until the fritters are crisp and golden. This will take about 6–7 minutes. Drain on paper towels. Serve immediately. Okra may also be simply dipped in milk and seasoned flour and deep-fried until golden. Quite delicious!

Garden Herb and Herb-Flower Salad with Basil Dressing and Parmesan Chips

SERVES 4 AS A FIRST COURSE
OR SIDE SALAD

16 leaves of mixed lettuce and salad greens—allow about 4 leaves per person

Sprigs of all or some of the following:
HERBS:
Mint, tarragon, dill, cilantro, fennel, basil, marjoram, thyme, flat-leaf parsley, chives

FLOWERS:
Chive, nasturtium, marigold, cilantro, zucchini

Parmesan Chips (see page 188)

BASIL DRESSING
2 tablespoons wine vinegar
6 tablespoons Basil Oil (see page 184)
$^1/_2$ teaspoon mustard (Dijon or prepared English)
I small clove garlic, minced
I small scallion
Sprig of parsley
Sprig of watercress
$^1/_2$ teaspoon salt
A pinch of sugar
A few grinds of black pepper

We have a huge wooden salad bowl in the School's dining room, turned from Irish elm by Keith Mosse. It is used every single day for as many as 50 people and is an important part of the School: the salad is different each day, and the students are continually fascinated when they go out in the morning with one of the gardeners to pick for it. In summer it overflows with lettuces, edible flowers, herbs, and little greens. We always list the contents on the blackboard—there can be up to 20 different ingredients. This more than anything seems to teach the students the potential of the garden. Many have forgotten the flavor of home-grown lettuce, as most commercial salad leaves are grown hydroponically and have less taste.

Wash all the salad leaves and, if necessary, the herbs and flowers. Process all the ingredients for the dressing in a blender for a few seconds. Or you can mix the oil and vinegar in a bowl, then add the mustard, salt, pepper, and garlic. Mince the parsley, scallion, and watercress and add. Whisk before serving.

Next make the Parmesan Chips.

Toss the leaves, herbs, and flowers in just enough dressing to make them glisten, and pile the salad on individual plates. Garnish with herb flowers and serve immediately with the Parmesan Chips.

(RIGHT) *Box* (Buxus sempervirens) *outlines the beautiful Celtic pattern of the herb garden which was inspired by a visit to Villandry in the Loire valley.*

Kinoith Summer Garden Salad

SERVES 4–6

A SELECTION OF:

butterhead lettuce, Oak Leaf lettuce, Little Gem lettuce, iceberg lettuce, radicchio, arugula, edible chrysanthe-mum leaves, sorrel leaves, golden marjoram, salad burnet, borage or hyssop flowers, young nasturtium leaves and flowers, marigold petals, chive or wild garlic flowers, herb leaves, such as lemon balm, mint, and flat-leaf parsley, green pea shoots, tiny ruby chard, spinach or beet greens, zucchini blossoms, or fava bean tips

HONEY AND HERB DRESSING
3/4 cup extra virgin olive oil
4 tablespoons cider vinegar
1 teaspoon Irish honey
1 clove garlic, minced
2 tablespoons chopped fresh mixed herbs (parsley, chives, mint, watercress, and thyme)
Salt and freshly ground black pepper

"Kinoith" is the name of our house and the location of the Cookery School. The name comes from the Celtic Ciún-áit or Cion-ait, which means "quiet" or "friendly place." It has now been anglicized as there is no K in the Celtic alphabet.

Wash" and dry the lettuce and salad greens. If large, tear into bite-sized bits. Put in a deep salad bowl and add the herb sprigs and edible flowers. Toss, then cover and chill for a few minutes.

To make the dressing, put all the ingredients into a jar, adding salt and pepper to taste. Cover tightly and shake well to emulsify. Otherwise, work all the ingredients in a food processor or blender for a few seconds.

As a variation you could use 3 tablespoons of fresh lemon juice or wine vinegar instead of cider vinegar.

Just before serving, toss the salad in just enough dressing to make the leaves glisten—save the remainder of the dressing for another day.

Shanagarry Tomato Salad

One variety or a mixture of very ripe vine-ripened tomatoes—try to include some cherry tomatoes, pear-shaped tomatoes, and, if you can get them, the striped ones that look and taste particularly wonderful

Sea salt and freshly ground black pepper
Sugar

Ballymaloe Vinaigrette (see page 182) or balsamic vinegar or white wine vinegar and extra virgin olive oil

GARNISH
Fresh basil leaves or mint leaves

Tomatoes have been grown in the greenhouses here in Shanagarry since my father-in-law, Ivan Allen, built his first timber house in the winter of 1934. For years the crops were grown commercially, but for the past eight to ten years we have concentrated on growing as many varieties as we have space for, with total emphasis on flavor—yield is not a high priority—and every tomato is ripened on the vine. Varieties we enjoy are Sweet 100, Green Zebra, Valencia, and Golden Jubilee. We even grow the tiny Tumbler variety, interspersed with herbs, in hanging baskets outside the cottages and around the school. Freshly picked, sweet-tasting tomatoes, piled high in baskets, are part of every day, and tomato salads, made from a mixture of colors, shapes, and varieties, are part of almost every menu in late summer and early autumn. Never store tomatoes in the refrigerator.

Cut the tomatoes in half or in wedges or simply into 1/4 inch thick slices, depending on the shape and size. Spread out in a single layer on a large flat plate and season with sea salt, pepper, and a little sugar. Sprinkle with Ballymaloe Vinaigrette, or, sparingly, with balsamic vinegar and generously with extra virgin olive oil. Scatter torn basil or mint leaves over. Toss gently, just to coat the tomatoes. Serve soon, either as a first course or as an accompanying salad.

Spinach with Raisins and Pine Nuts

SERVES 6

1/4 cup good seedless raisins
1/4 cup fresh pine nuts
3 pounds fresh spinach
4 tablespoons butter
2 tablespoons extra virgin olive oil
Salt and freshly ground black pepper
A splash of balsamic vinegar

We grow perpetual spinach year round and annual spinach through the summer season. We use it in soups, salads, toppings for pizzas, and as a vegetable—wilted, sautéed, and puréed. It creates the green in pasta verde, and the tiny succulent new leaves are a "must have" in our summer green salads. For this recipe I prefer to use melting summer spinach, but you could also use perpetual spinach with its slightly stronger flavor and more robust texture. It is particularly delicious with Baby Beef Scaloppine (page 73) or Roast Pork with Spiced Eggplant (page 120).

Put the raisins into a little bowl and cover them with boiling water. Let soak for about 10 minutes so they become plump and juicy. Drain.

Meanwhile, toast the pine nuts until they are golden brown. Remove the coarse stems from the spinach, wash well in several changes of cold water, and drain. Cook in a large covered saucepan with no liquid apart from that

which adheres to the leaves after washing. Cook over medium heat and toss once or twice. As soon as the leaves are tender, drain thoroughly and squeeze dry. Mince the spinach.

Melt the butter and oil in a sauté pan and add the spinach, raisins, and pine nuts. Season well with salt and pepper. Allow to bubble for 4–5 minutes, then add a splash of balsamic vinegar. Taste and correct the seasoning. Serve immediately.

Whole Roasted Garlic

SERVES 6–10

I pound whole garlic bulbs—6–10, depending on size
2¹/₂ cups extra virgin olive oil
Salt and freshly ground black pepper
I–2 sprigs fresh thyme, rosemary, or sage (optional)

Save the leftover oil, which will be deliciously flavored with roasted garlic, to use in other dishes.

Preheat the oven to 350°F.

Slice the top quarter off each bulb of garlic with a sharp knife. Arrange the garlic bulbs in a single layer in a shallow baking pan—we use a lasagne dish. Pour the olive oil over and season with salt and pepper. I sometimes tuck in a sprig or two of thyme, rosemary, or sage. Cover with aluminum foil and bake for about an hour, by which time the garlic cloves will be beginning to pop out of their skins. Discard the foil and bake, uncovered, for a further I5–20 minutes or until golden brown.

Globe Artichoke Bottoms Braised in Olive Oil

SERVES 4

1 lemon
6 globe artichokes
6 tablespoons extra virgin olive oil
1 onion, coarsely diced
2 cloves garlic, chopped
4 tablespoons coarsely chopped parsley
Salt and freshly ground black pepper

Ireland has a great climate for globe artichokes. Fields of them make one of the more bizarre sights that greet tourists on the Beara peninsula. Our variety has been handed down through generations of Myrtle Allen's family. We mostly eat them whole, dripping with melted butter or Hollandaise. We grow so many that by the time August comes, we get more flahulach *with them and just eat the artichoke bottoms.*

Preparing the artichokes is the fiddliest part of this recipe. Acidulate a large bowl of water with the juice of the lemon. Drop in the squeezed lemon halves too, for good measure. Cut a ring around the stalk of the artichoke where it meets the base. Break off the stalk and the toughest fibers will come with it. Then, with a sharp knife, starting from the base, ruthlessly cut off all the leaves and trim the top down as far as the fleshy bottom. Scrape out the hairy choke, either with the tip of a knife or a sharp-edged spoon. Work quickly, and drop the trimmed bottoms into the acidulated water immediately, or they will discolor.

Heat the oil in a wide sauté pan, add the chopped onion and garlic, and sweat for a few minutes. Cut the drained artichoke bottoms into quarters or eighths and add to the pan with the chopped parsley. Season with salt and freshly ground pepper and toss well.

Kohlrabi with Marjoram

SERVES 4–6

1 pound kohlrabi
Butter
Salt and freshly ground white pepper
Fresh annual marjoram

We grow both green- and purple-skinned kohlrabi; they are a wonderfully delicate vegetable and deserve to be better known. Use them while they are still young, not much bigger than a golf ball. Like turnips, they become woody as they get larger or if the summer is very dry.

Peel the kohlrabi and slice it thickly. Melt the butter in a flameproof casserole and toss in the kohlrabi until it is barely coated. Season with salt and pepper. Add a tablespoon of water and a sprig of marjoram. Cover with buttered parchment paper and the lid of the casserole. Cook over low heat for 8–10 minutes or until the kohlrabi is just tender. Remove the cooked herbs and add a little freshly chopped marjoram. Taste and correct the seasoning, then serve. Watch the amount of marjoram so as not to overpower the delectable but delicate flavor of the kohlrabi.

Fresh Apricot Tart

SERVES 10–12

PASTRY

I²/₃ cups all-purpose flour
³/₄ cup (I¹/₂ sticks) butter
Pinch of salt
2 teaspoons confectioners' sugar
A little beaten free-range egg or egg yolk
and water

APRICOT GLAZE

6 tablespoons apricot jam
Freshly squeezed lemon juice

FILLING

8–10 fresh apricots
2 extra large or 3 medium eggs
2 tablespoons sugar
I teaspoon pure vanilla extract
I¹/₄ cups heavy cream

YOU WILL NEED

A 12-inch tart pan or 2 7-inch tart pans
with removable bases

This is my version of a tart I first tasted when I was a rather reluctant au pair in France many years ago; it is now one of our favorites. Apples, pears, gooseberries, rhubarb, and plums are also good, and the custard could be flavored with a little cinnamon instead of vanilla if you want to ring the changes.

Preheat the oven to 350°F.

Make the pastry in the usual way (see page 183) and let it relax in the refrigerator for 1 hour. Roll out the pastry and line the tart pan (or pans). Chill for 10 minutes. Line with wax paper and fill with dried beans. Bake in the preheated oven for 15–20 minutes. Remove the wax paper and beans. Paint the bottom of the tart shell with a little egg wash and return to the oven to bake for 3 or 4 minutes. Let cool.

In a small stainless steel saucepan, melt the apricot jam with a squeeze of lemon juice. Push the hot jam through a strainer. Brush the bottom of the tart shell with a little of the glaze.

Halve the apricots and remove the pits. Arrange, cut-side up, in the tart shell; the apricots should slightly overlap.

Whisk the eggs well with the sugar and vanilla, then add the cream. Pour this mixture over the apricots. Bake in the preheated oven for 35 minutes or until the custard is set and the apricots are fully cooked. Brush generously with the apricot glaze, and serve warm with a bowl of softly whipped cream.

Summer Berries with Sweet Geranium Leaves

SERVES 8–10

1 cup raspberries
1 cup loganberries
1 cup red currants
1 cup black currants
1 cup strawberries
1 cup blueberries
3/4 cup fraises des bois (wild strawberries)—optional

SYRUP
2 cups sugar
2 cups water
6–8 large sweet geranium leaves

DECORATION
Sweet geranium leaves

Sweet geranium (Pelargonium graveolens) and many other varieties of scented geraniums are ever present on our windowsills here at Ballymaloe. We use the delicious lemon-scented leaves in all sorts of ways. Occasionally, we also use the pretty purple flowers to enliven and add magic to otherwise simple dishes. The leaves can be crystallized and are wonderful with fresh cream cheese and fat juicy blackberries. I discovered this recipe, which has now become a perennial favorite, quite by accident a few summers ago as I raced to make a dessert in a hurry with the ingredients I had at that moment.

Put all the freshly picked berries into a serving bowl. Put the sugar, cold water, and sweet geranium leaves into a stainless steel saucepan and bring slowly to a bowl, stirring until the sugar dissolves. Boil for just 2 minutes. Pour the boiling syrup over the fruit, then let macerate for several hours. Remove the geranium leaves. Serve chilled, with softly whipped cream, Vanilla Ice Cream (see page 173), or on its own. Decorate with a few fresh sweet geranium leaves.

Honey Lavender Ice Cream

SERVES 8–10

1 cup milk
2 cups heavy cream
40 sprigs fresh lavender or less of dried
(use the blossom end only)
6 free-range egg yolks
3/4 cup pure Irish honey—we use
our own apple blossom honey,
although Provençal lavender honey
would also be wonderful

DECORATION
Sprigs of lavender

I make this richly scented ice cream in June, when the lavender flowers in the kitchen garden bloom. Lavender is at its most aromatic just before the flowers open. Serve it on its own on chilled plates and savor every mouthful.

Put the milk and cream into a heavy saucepan with the lavender sprigs. Bring slowly to a boil, then let infuse for 15–20 minutes. This will both flavor and perfume the liquid deliciously. Whisk the egg yolks, add a little of the lavender-flavored liquid, and then mix the two together. Cook over low heat until the mixture barely thickens and lightly coats the back of a spoon (be careful that it does not curdle). Warm the honey gently—just to liquefy—and whisk into the custard. Strain out the lavender heads. Chill thoroughly, then freeze, preferably in an ice cream machine.

Serve decorated with sprigs of lavender.

Carrageen-Moss Pudding with Crushed Blueberries

SERVES 4–6

1/2 cup cleaned, well-dried carrageen moss (1 semi-closed fistful)
3 1/2 cups half-and-half
1/2 teaspoon pure vanilla extract or a vanilla bean
1 egg, preferably free-range
1 heaping tablespoon sugar

Blueberries or, better still, wild bilberries or *fraughans*
Granulated sugar
Softly whipped cream
Brown sugar

Carrageen moss is bursting with goodness. I ate it as a child, but never liked it, as it was always too stiff and unpalatable. Myrtle Allen changed my opinion! Hers was always so light and fluffy. I even had it for our wedding feast, made with fraughans *(bilberries). Alas, the dye from the fraughans dyed all the guests' gums purple, to the consternation of our photographer.*

Soak the carrageen in tepid water for 10 minutes. Strain off the water and put the carrageen into a saucepan with the half-and-half and vanilla bean, if used. Bring to a boil, then cover and simmer very gently for 20 minutes. At that point, and not before, separate the egg and put the yolk into a bowl. Add the sugar and vanilla extract and whisk together for a few seconds. Pour the carrageen moss mixture through a strainer onto the egg yolk mixture, whisking all the time. The carrageen will now be swollen and exuding jelly. Rub all this jelly through the strainer and beat it into the flavored half-and-half. Test for a set in a saucer as one would jelly or jam. If it is a little soft, add a little of the strained-out liquid and push more carrageen through the strainer.

Whisk the egg white stiffly and fold it in gently with a whisk. It will rise to make a fluffy top. Let cool, then chill until set.

Just before serving, crush the blueberries slightly with a potato masher, sprinkle generously with granulated sugar, and mix well. Serve the carrageen pudding with the berries and cream and a sprinkle of brown sugar, for a divine combination of flavors.

Peach and Raspberry Crisp

SERVES ABOUT 8

I cup all-purpose flour
I cup packed light brown sugar
$3^1/_2$ cups organic oat flakes
$^1/_4$ teaspoon freshly ground nutmeg
$^1/_3$ teaspoon ground cinnamon
I cup (2 sticks) butter, melted

2 pounds peaches or nectarines
3 cups raspberries
I tablespoon cornstarch

In the summer of 1996, I spent a few days at Zingermann's deli in Ann Arbor, Michigan. They make sensational sandwiches, salads, and desserts. Ari Weinzweig sent me a recipe for this delicious pudding.

Preheat the oven to 350°F.

Put all the dry ingredients into a bowl, add the melted butter, and mix until crumbly. Slice the peaches into a baking dish measuring about $10^1/_2$ by $9^1/_2$ inches. Add the raspberries. Sprinkle with the cornstarch and mix well. If the fruit is unusually tart you may need to add a little sugar. Top with a generous and even layer of the oat mixture. (I keep the rest for another day to use with plums.)

Bake in the preheated oven for 30–40 minutes or until the topping is crisp and the fruit tender. The juices should bubble up around the edges. Serve with softly whipped cream.

Lemon Verbena and Lemon Balm Sorbet

SERVES ABOUT 8

I cup plus 2 tablespoons sugar
$2^1/_2$ cups cold water
2 large handfuls of lemon verbena and lemon balm leaves
Freshly squeezed juice of 3 lemons
I free-range egg white (optional)

DECORATION
Lemon verbena and lemon balm leaves

Rory O'Connell, my brother, serves this deliciously fresh sorbet as a first course at Ballymaloe House; it just flits across the tongue and scarcely needs to be swallowed. A perfect start to a late summer meal.

If you don't have an ice cream machine, simply freeze the sorbet in a bowl in the freezer. When it is semi-frozen, whisk until smooth and return to the freezer again. Whisk again when almost fully frozen, and fold in one stiffly beaten egg white. Keep in the freezer until needed. If you have a food processor, simply freeze the sorbet completely in a baking pan, then break up and work for a few seconds in the processor. Drop one slightly beaten egg white into the processor, process again, and freeze. Serve as below.

Put the first three ingredients into a non-metal saucepan and bring to a boil slowly. Simmer for 2–3 minutes. Then leave to get quite cold. Add the lemon juice. Strain and freeze for 20–25 minutes in an ice cream machine. Serve in chilled glasses or chilled china bowls. Decorate with lemon verbena and lemon balm leaves.

Meringue Roulade with Summer Strawberries and Fresh Raspberry Sauce

SERVES 6

4 free-range egg whites
1 cup plus 2 tablespoons superfine sugar
1¼ cups heavy cream
¾-1 pound fresh strawberries

RASPBERRY SAUCE
6–8 tablespoons Stock Syrup (page 93)
2 cups raspberries
Lemon juice (optional)

DECORATION
6 whole strawberries
Free-range egg white
Sugar
Sprigs of fresh mint, lemon balm, or
sweet cicely

YOU WILL NEED
A 12- by 8-inch baking pan

This delectable roulade is also very good filled with raspberries, loganberries, sliced peaches, nectarines, kiwi fruit, or sliced bananas tossed in lemon juice.

Preheat the oven to 350°F.

Put the egg whites into the spotlessly clean bowl of an electric mixer. Break up with the beaters, then add the sugar. Beat at full speed until the meringue holds a stiff peak, about 4–5 minutes.

Meanwhile, line the pan with aluminum foil and brush lightly with a non-scented oil, such as sunflower or peanut. Spread the meringue gently in the pan with a metal spatula—it should be quite thick and bouncy.

Bake in the preheated oven for 15–20 minutes. Put a sheet of foil on the work top and turn the roulade onto it. Remove the foil lining carefully and let the meringue cool.

Purée the raspberries and stock syrup in a blender or food processor. Press through a fine-mesh strainer. Taste and sharpen with lemon juice if necessary. Store in the refrigerator.

To assemble, spread the whipped cream over the meringue. Slice the strawberries and mix with a little of the raspberry sauce. Spread the fruit on the meringue. Roll up from a narrow end and ease carefully onto a serving plate.

Dip the 6 whole strawberries in a very little egg white and sprinkle with sugar. Pipe six rosettes of whipped cream along the top of the roulade. Decorate with the sugared strawberries, or just fresh strawberries, and herb leaves.

Serve cut into slices about 1 inch thick, accompanied by the remaining raspberry sauce.

Loganberry Tart or Tartlets

SERVES 12

$^1/_2$ cup (I stick) butter
$^1/_2$ cup plus I tablespoon sugar
I$^1/_3$ cups ground almonds (use the best
you can afford)
4–6 tablespoons red-currant jelly
I pound loganberries (or use raspberries,
poached rhubarb, sliced peaches or
nectarines, peeled seedless grapes, or
kiwi fruit)

DECORATION

Lemon balm or sweet geranium leaves

I$^1/_4$ cups heavy cream

YOU WILL NEED

2 7-inch layer cake pans or 24 tiny
tartlet molds

This crisp almond tart base takes just minutes to make and is particularly delicious with tangy berries or carefully poached rhubarb.

Preheat the oven to 350°F.

Cream the butter with the sugar. Add the ground almonds and mix just long enough to bring the ingredients together. Divide the mixture between the layer cake pans or put a teaspoon of mixture into each of the tartlet molds. Bake in the preheated oven for about 20–30 minutes or until golden brown.

The tarts or tartlets will be too soft to unmold immediately, so let cool for about 5 minutes before removing from the pans. Do not let them set hard or the butter will solidify and they will stick to the pans. If this happens, put the pans back into the oven for a few minutes so the butter melts, and then they will come out easily. Let cool on a wire rack.

Just before serving, arrange the whole loganberries on the bases and glaze with red-currant jelly. Pipe a little whipped cream around the edge and decorate with lemon balm or sweet geranium leaves.

Fraises des Bois Ice Cream with Strawberry and Rhubarb Compote

Rhubarb and strawberries marry wonderfully, and now that strawberries have a longer season, we can enjoy them together. The secret to cooking rhubarb for a compote is to let it boil for just the briefest cooking. Unlike plums, gooseberries, or apricots, the fruit must keep its shape. This compote is fabulous for breakfast. Serve it icy cold.

First make the ice cream. Dissolve the sugar in the water and boil for 7–10 minutes, then let cool. Purée the strawberries in a food processor or blender and press through a fine-mesh strainer. Add the orange and lemon juices to the cold syrup. Stir into the purée, then fold in the whipped cream. Freeze immediately in an ice cream machine according to the manufacturer's instructions.

SERVES 6

FRAISES DES BOIS ICE CREAM
I cup plus 2 tablespoons sugar
I^1/$_4$ cups water
2 pounds very ripe fraises des bois
(wild strawberries)
Juice of ^{1}/$_2$ orange
Juice of ^{1}/$_2$ lemon
^{2}/$_3$ cup heavy cream, whipped

STRAWBERRY AND RHUBARB
COMPOTE
I pound rhubarb
2 cups Stock Syrup (see below)

^{1}/$_2$–I pound fresh strawberries

DECORATION
Fresh mint or lemon balm leaves

STOCK SYRUP
2^1/$_4$ cups sugar
2^1/$_2$ cups water
Dissolve the sugar in the water and bring
to a boil. Boil for 2 minutes, then let
cool. Store in the refrigerator until
needed.

Next make the compote. Cut the rhubarb into 1-inch pieces. Put the cold stock syrup into a stainless steel saucepan and add the rhubarb. Cover the pan, bring to a boil, and simmer for 1 minute. Remove from the heat and leave the rhubarb in the covered saucepan until just cold. The fruit will be tender and plump. Hull the strawberries; leave them whole or slice lengthwise. Add them to the rhubarb compote.

To serve: scoop out the ice cream into a pretty glass bowl and serve with the chilled compote. Decorate with fresh mint or lemon balm leaves.

Homemade Cheese with Fresh Herbs and Crackers

MAKES ABOUT I POUND CHEESE

2^1/$_2$ quarts whole milk
^{1}/$_2$ teaspoon liquid rennet (you can get vegetarian rennet, too)

YOU WILL NEED
Good-quality muslin or cheesecloth

HOMEMADE CRACKERS
MAKES 25–30

I cup whole wheat flour
^{3}/$_4$ cup all-purpose flour, preferably unbleached
^{1}/$_2$ teaspoon salt
^{1}/$_2$ teaspoon baking powder
2 tablespoons butter
5–6 tablespoons cream

2–4 tablespoons chopped fresh herbs (parsley, chives, chervil, lemon balm, and perhaps a little tarragon and thyme)
2–3 cloves garlic, minced (optional)
Salt and freshly ground black pepper

This is super-easy to make, and people are bowled over with admiration when you produce homemade cheese and crackers.

Put the milk into a spotlessly clean, stainless steel saucepan. Heat it very gently until it reaches the "shivery" stage and is barely tepid. Add the rennet, stirring it well into the milk.

Cover the saucepan with a clean dish towel and the lid. (The dish towel prevents the steam from condensing on the lid of the pan and falling back onto the curd.) Set aside and leave undisturbed somewhere in your kitchen for 2–4 hours, by which time the milk should have coagulated and will be solid.

Cut the curd into dice with a spotlessly clean knife. Put back on very low heat and warm gently until the whey starts to run out of the curds. It must not get hot or the curd will tighten and toughen too much. Ladle into a cheesecloth-lined colander set over a bowl. Tie the corners of the cloth together and let drip overnight.

To make the crackers, preheat the oven to 350°F.

Mix the flours together and add the salt and baking powder. Cut in the butter and moisten with enough cream to make a firm dough. Roll out very thinly—about ^{1}/$_{16}$ inch thick. Prick with a fork and cut into 2^1/$_2$-inch squares, diamonds, or rounds. Bake in the preheated oven for 20–25 minutes or until lightly browned and quite crisp. Cool on a wire rack.

Press the cheese through a fine-mesh strainer. Mix in the freshly chopped herbs and garlic, if using. Season to taste. It may even need a pinch of sugar. Spoon the cheese into a pretty bowl and serve with the homemade crackers.

Lemon-Grass Lemonade

MAKES ABOUT 5 CUPS

SYRUP
2¹/₂ cups water
2¹/₂ cups sugar
2 stems lemon grass, finely sliced

FOR THE LEMONADE
3 lemons
3–4 cups water

If you live in a rural area, or indeed far from a good greengrocer, and you want to have access to exotic ingredients, the only solution is to grow your own. That is what we did with lemon grass, and now we have so much that we can afford to use it liberally in all sorts of ways, for instance in this refreshing and delicious drink.

First make the syrup. Put the cold water and sugar into a saucepan with the finely sliced lemon grass. Bring the mixture slowly to a boil and simmer for 2 minutes. Let cool. Strain out the lemon grass.

When the syrup is cold, juice the lemons and mix the freshly squeezed juice with the water and 1 cup of the lemon-grass syrup. Keep the remaining syrup in the refrigerator for another day. Mix well and taste, then dilute with more water if necessary.

Serve chilled.

Tisanes

Fresh herbs (such as lemon verbena, rosemary, sweet geranium, lemon balm, spearmint, or peppermint)

We make lots of fresh herb infusions. If you have fresh herbs, all you need to do is put a few leaves into a teapot and pour on the boiling water—infinitely more delicious. I have a particular aversion to the little tea bags that are frequently used. I am very wary about ordering herbal tea in a restaurant for this reason, but one Paris restaurant where I dined recently served herb infusions in the most delightful way. The waiter came to the table with several china bowls of fresh herbs on a silver salver. With tiny tongs he put the guests' chosen herb into a little china teapot, poured on boiling water, and served it with a flourish. Exquisite.

Bring fresh cold water to a boil. Warm a china teapot. Take a handful of fresh herb leaves and crush them gently in your hand. The quantity will depend on the strength of the herb and how intense an infusion you enjoy. Put them into the teapot. Pour the boiling water over the leaves, cover the teapot, and let infuse for 3–4 minutes. Serve immediately in china cups.

Autumn

As soon as the September students settle in, I take them foraging. Autumn is the best time for this. They think I'm crazy, but I tell them how foraging is all the rage on the West Coast of America. Chez Panisse in Berkeley has its own forager, as have The Herb Farm in Seattle and Sooke Harbour House on Vancouver Island. We go along the hedgerows into the fields and onto the beach, where we find a multitude of things like damsons, sloes, blueberries, blackberries, seaweeds, samphire, sorrel, wild mushrooms, periwinkles, and mussels. They learn to make blackberry jam and damson jam. We make crab-apple jelly with sweet geranium leaves, and rich elderberry jelly. We make sorrel soup and we're probably the only people in the area who collect seaweed from the strand (beach): years ago there were pitched battles over the seaweed, before artificial fertilizers became widely available.

We introduce the students to the gardens and the gardeners who grow the produce they will cook. I talk to them about growing organically. If I had it my way, all the surrounding farmland beyond our hundred acres would be organic, too. We use no artificial fertilizers; just compost, manure, peat moss, and seaweed. Elizabeth O'Connell, Haulie Walsh, and Eileen O'Donovan look after the gardens. The vegetable garden was laid out painstakingly, with old brick herringbone paths, by Frank Walsh in 1989, and it is now a formal pattern, a diamond bisected by a cross, filled with a delicious and hugely varied array of vegetables, such a treat to harvest in the early autumn. It is designed to be decorative as well as functional. But what happens now that everything is planted in patterns? Sometimes I can scarcely bear to cut a lettuce for fear of ruining the symmetry! In the garden we seem to be able to grow pretty much anything we want—grapes, almonds, Asian pears, olives, figs, nectarines, as well as mulberries, cranberries, and blueberries. We've also grown chiles successfully outside, and Asian vegetables: bok choy, mizuna, mustard greens, and garland chrysanthemum leaves. In the greenhouses, there's still lots of lemon grass and many different varieties of tomatoes, cucumbers, and all sorts of beans.

Ollie and Iris from Manch Farm supply us with organic sheep's milk ricotta, Orla cheese, and thick, delicious yogurt. Ina Korner brings goat-milk yogurt and cheese from near Youghal; all the people work like mad to produce these exquisite foods. We are fortunate to have a network of fantastic suppliers and the whole locality can benefit from their brilliance. I feel so deeply grateful to all artisanal producers. We must all support them to help them flourish.

(LEFT) *Behind the house and gardens at Kinoith is pastureland, grazed by our Kerry cows.*

(RIGHT) *We grow teazels* (Dipsacus fullonum) *for their striking cheerfulness in later winter flower decorations.*

On the three-month courses, the students meet the gardeners each morning on a rota basis, to pick the herbs and fruit and vegetables; on the short courses, that's an option if they are very keen. This is certainly one of the things that makes this cookery school pretty much unique for many people. It's also something that our guest chefs greatly enjoy. Many of my culinary idols have taught here: Madhur Jaffrey, Claudia Roden, Jane Grigson, Marcella Hazan, Sri Owen.

My culinary influences come from so many different people. I think immediately of the late Elizabeth David—so many of her recipes are completely delicious and still retain their currency even when times change. Julia Child, too, is a great influence. I learned much from my mother, Elizabeth O'Connell, whose cooking I took totally for granted as a child. Then, of course, Myrtle Allen, my mother-in-law, has always been, and continues to be, a huge inspiration; I find her to be a visionary, yet overwhelmingly modest. She has a tremendous confidence that allows her to cook as she wants with no regard for the latest fleeting fashion.

(BELOW) *The fruit garden may give the Cookery School students their first real opportunity to pick fruit straight from the trees, and we try to make them aware of the abundance of wild food, and the excitement of foraging.*

(ABOVE) *The vegetable garden, where the tones of the beach hedge in autumn blend well with those of the Whichford pots, which are used to force seakale. The marvelous ironwork around the School is made by our local blacksmith, Andy Grierson.*

I've been collecting old roses for several years. Richard Wood has given me many and they've been sitting around in tubs while I plan my rose garden, which I hope will eventually be in the old orchard. I also have plans for an Irish Garden with an emblem for each of the four provinces—the red hand of Ulster, the harp of Leinster, the three crowns for Munster, and the eagle and sword for Connaught. I adore eighteenth-century gardens and long to do a double beech circle with a pond in the center like the one I saw at Kilruddery outside Dublin. Such beautiful gardens. And I want to plant the Irish Apple Collection. There would

certainly be over a hundred, maybe more. Always plans! I feel terribly fortunate that we inherited Kinoith, even though the gardens were a wilderness for a time. If someone hadn't planted them back in the 1830s I would never have had a base to restore and build on, so, to a certain extent, I am giving much back to Kinoith by planting for the next generation. I hope that the gardens catch my children's imaginations; it would be great if they could give even one member of the family tremendous pleasure.

I saw a herd of Kerry cows when traveling around Ireland with my TV crew, filming for Irish television. So I bought an in-calf heifer from an organic farmer, Ivan Ward, who has now become a friend and advisor. Eileen, one of my garden angels and a farmer's daughter from West Cork, had the misfortune to say she could milk a cow. Haulie, who helps us in the gardens, holds the cow at one end and Eileen milks it at the other. In the autumn, the cows appear to shake the apple trees in the orchard while the pigs stand underneath munching the apples that fall. I was so disenchanted with the quality of pork that I bought a couple of saddlebacks. They needed a mate so I bought a Berkshire boar from a man I met up walking in the Comeragh mountains. As a result, Black Pudding, as he is called, is a daddy and we had Rasher and Sausage. Sausage went off to be made into sausages. We've had lots and lots of litters since then and they are happy, lazy pigs. Pigs reared in intensive units have nothing in the world to recommend them and their meat has no flavor. We don't feel that we have the right to keep animals unless they are comfortable and have humane conditions. I feel this very, very strongly and, though I have no wish to be a vegetarian, I do not want to eat meat from animals that have just had a horrible life from start to finish.

(ABOVE) *Chervil and Rocket (our donkeys) were a present from the students of one of 1996's three-month courses.*

(LEFT) *The "Palais de Poulets" is home to our extensive collection of hens. Frank and JP collect their eggs, which we then use in the School. The taste, for some people, is a forgotten flavor.*

(RIGHT) *All our pigs lead a happy life, which leads, in the end, to sweeter pork.*

Fresh Tomato Juice

SERVES ABOUT 4–6

SERVES ABOUT 4–6

1 pound very ripe tomatoes, peeled
and halved
1 scallion with a little green leaf, or
1 slice onion, 2 inches diameter and $^1/_4$
inch thick
3 large fresh basil leaves or 5–6 mint leaves
2 teaspoons white wine vinegar
1 tablespoon olive oil
$^1/_2$ cup water
1 teaspoon salt
1 teaspoon sugar
A few grinds of black pepper

This is only worth making when you have very well-flavored vine-ripened tomatoes. We make it throughout September when our tomatoes have really developed intense flavor. It is best when freshly made and better not kept for more than 8 hours. It makes a great base for Bloody Mary's, or you can sweeten it and freeze it as a granita.

Blend the ingredients together, then strain through a nylon strainer. Taste and add more seasoning if necessary. Serve unadorned in tall glasses.

Wild Mushroom Soup

SERVES 8–9

$^3/_4$ cup minced onion
3 tablespoons butter
1 pound fresh wild mushrooms
Salt and freshly ground black pepper
3 tablespoons all-purpose flour
$2^1/_2$ cups Homemade Chicken Stock
(see page 184)
$2^1/_2$ cups milk
Dash of cream (optional)

Some years pass and not a single mushroom pops up in the fields; in other years they are so abundant that we are frantically making ketchup, sauces, soups, and so on to use them up. In fact, the base of this recipe is a perfect way to preserve wild mushrooms when local children bring us more than we can eat: let the mixture (without the stock) cool, then freeze it.

Melt the butter in a saucepan on a gentle heat. Toss the onion in it, then cover and sweat until soft and completely cooked. Meanwhile, mince the mushrooms. (If you can't be bothered to mince the mushrooms, just slice and then process the soup in a blender for a few seconds after it is cooked.) Add the mushrooms to the saucepan and cook on high heat for 3–4 minutes. Then stir in the flour and cook on low heat for 2–3 minutes. Season with salt and pepper,. Add the stock and milk gradually, stirring all the time. Increase the heat and bring to a boil. Taste and add a dash of cream if necessary, then serve.

Beet Soup with Chive Cream

SERVES 8–10

1³/₄ pounds beets
1¹/₂ cups chopped onions
2 tablespoons butter
Salt and freshly ground black pepper
About 5 cups Homemade Chicken Stock
(see page 184)
Cream

CHIVE CREAM
¹/₂ cup sour cream, softly whipped
Minced fresh chives

We love beets in all shapes and forms. In the spring, we eat them when they are tiny, with butter, cream, and parsley. We also adore the tiny leaves in salads, and use the larger ones as wilted greens with garlic and olive oil. The larger beets (golden Chioggia is an excellent variety) we pickle or make into soups, or simply bake in the oven. One fabulous use for them is to make chips (see page 127 for vegetable chips).

Wash the beets carefully under a cold tap. Don't scrub; simply rub off the soil with your fingers—you don't want to damage the skin or cut off the top or root because the beets will "bleed" in the cooking. Put the beets into boiling water and simmer, covered, for anything from 20 minutes to 2 hours, depending on the size. The beets are cooked when the skins will rub off easily.

Meanwhile, sweat the onions gently in the butter until they are soft. Chop the beets and add to the onions. Season with salt and pepper. Put into a blender with the chicken stock. Blend until quite smooth. Reheat, add a little cream, and taste and adjust the seasoning—it may be necessary to add a little more stock or cream. Serve garnished with swirls of whipped sour cream and a sprinkling of chives.

Pumpkin Soup

SERVES 6–8

2 pounds (8 cups) pumpkin flesh, cut in
small cubes
4 tablespoons butter
2 onions, sliced
2 teaspoons chopped fresh marjoram
or thyme
Salt and freshly ground black pepper
1–1^1/$_2$ tablespoons sugar
2^1/$_2$ cups milk
About 1^1/$_4$ cups Homemade Chicken
Stock (see page 184) (optional)

GARNISH
4 slices bacon
2 heaping tablespoons whipped cream
1 tablespoon chopped parsley

Pumpkins grow so well in our vegetable garden, and we harvest them in October and November. We grow several varieties and many kinds of squash, too, so they are used in many more ways than simply becoming lanterns at Halloween.

The method you use to prepare the pumpkin will depend on how you intend to serve the soup. If you plan to serve it in a tureen or individual soup bowls, simply cut the pumpkin in half or quarters and scoop out the seeds and fibrous matter from the center. Save the seeds to roast (see below) and nibble as a snack. Peel off the skin with a knife and cut the flesh into cubes.

If, however, you would like to use the pumpkin shell for a more dramatic presentation, then you will need to proceed with care. Slice a "lid" off the top of the pumpkin and scoop out the seeds and fibrous matter. Then carefully scoop out the pumpkin flesh—a sharp-edged tablespoon is best for this, but be careful not to damage the pumpkin shell. You may need to make double the given quantities of soup to fill the pumpkin tureen.

Next make the soup. Melt the butter in a saucepan; when it foams, add the onions and sweat for a few minutes until soft. Add the pumpkin flesh and stir to coat in the butter. Add the herbs, salt, pepper, sugar, and milk. Bring to a boil and simmer until the pumpkin is cooked.

Purée in a blender, then taste and correct the seasoning if necessary. If the soup is a little thick, thin with some boiling chicken stock.

Cook the bacon slices until they are crisp, then crumble coarsley. Pour the hot soup into a tureen or back into the pumpkin shell and swirl the whipped cream on top. Scatter with crisp bacon and chopped parsley. Serve immediately.

Lydia's Roasted Pumpkin Seeds

Pumpkin seeds
Sea salt

Preheat the oven to 225°F.

Remove all the seeds from the flesh and rinse under cold water. Pat dry on paper towels. Lay in a single layer on a baking sheet and sprinkle generously with sea salt.

Roast in the preheated oven for 30–40 minutes until the seeds are nice and crunchy. They may be stored, sealed in a tin or a jar.

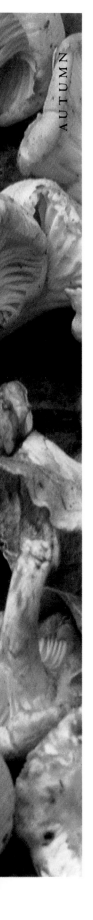

Fish Mousse with Chanterelles and Chive-Butter Sauce

SERVES 16–20

MOUSSE
³/₄ pound very fresh fillets of whiting or pollack, skinned and totally free of bone or membrane
I teaspoon salt
Pinch of freshly ground white pepper
I free-range egg
I free-range egg white
3 cups heavy cream, chilled

CHIVE-BUTTER SAUCE
Beurre Blanc (recipe x 2) (see page 29)
¹/₂–³/₄ pound fresh chanterelles
2 tablespoons butter
Salt and freshly ground black pepper
I–2 tablespoons minced chives

GARNISH
Sprigs of fresh chervil

YOU WILL NEED
16–20 ramekins—2¹/₂ fluid ounce capacity, 2 inch diameter, I inch deep

This recipe makes a large number of light fish mousses—it is difficult to reduce the quantities further without upsetting the proportions, so the recipe is perfect for a large dinner party. Even though the mousse is light, it is also very rich, so we cook it in small ramekins. The freshest sweet fish is utterly essential, because there is nothing to mask the taint if the fish is even slightly stale. The fish itself does not need to be expensive—we use pollack or whiting. Careful seasoning of the raw mixture is vital. Cooked crab meat, oysters, shrimp, periwinkles, or tiny dice of cucumber could also be added to the Beurre Blanc.

It is best to have everything well chilled to start with, including the bowl of the food processor. Cut the fish fillets into small dice and purée the pieces in the chilled bowl. Add the salt and pepper, then the egg and egg white; continue to process until these are well incorporated. Chill in the refrigerator for 30 minutes.

Preheat the oven to 400°F.

When the fish has chilled for 30 minutes, blend in the cream and process again just until it is well incorporated. Check the seasoning. The mousses can be prepared to this point several hours ahead. Cover and refrigerate until needed.

Brush the ramekins with melted butter. Spoon the mousse mixture into the ramekins and put them in a water bath of boiling water—it should come more than halfway up the ramekins. Cover with a pricked sheet of aluminum foil or wax paper and transfer to the preheated oven to bake for about 20 minutes. When cooked the mousses should feel just firm in the center. They will keep perfectly for 20–30 minutes in a plate-warming oven.

Meanwhile, make the Beurre Blanc in a heatproof bowl. Set the bowl in a saucepan of hot but not simmering water to keep warm.

Wash and slice the chanterelles. Melt the butter over high heat until it foams. Add the chanterelles and keep the heat turned up until they are cooked through. Season with salt and pepper, and add to the Beurre Blanc with the chives. Taste and correct the seasoning: the sauce should be very thin and light.

To serve: pour a little hot sauce onto each plate, unmold a mousse, and place it in the center. Arrange a few pieces of chanterelle around the wobbly mousse. Spoon a little more sauce over the mousse and serve immediately—they are no longer as delicious if they are allowed to get cold. Garnish with sprigs of chervil.

Oysters Chez Panisse

SERVES 4

A selection of lettuces and salad greens
16 fresh oysters

LEMON OIL DRESSING
1 large shallot, minced
1 tablespoon orange juice
1 tablespoon lemon juice
Salt and freshly ground black pepper
2 tablespoons wine or champagne vinegar
$^3/_4$ cup extra virgin olive oil
Grated zest of $^1/_2$ lemon
Grated zest of $^1/_2$ orange

All-purpose flour seasoned with salt and pepper
Beaten egg
White fluffy bread crumbs
Clarified butter

GARNISH
Snipped fresh flat-leaf parsley

Eddie Walsh, a chef at Ballymaloe House, goes to Chez Panisse in Berkeley, California, every year, to soak up Alice Waters' fresh exciting food philosophy. In the spring he returns to Ireland with his head swirling with ideas; and after one such trip he cooked me these oysters.

Wash and dry the lettuces and salad greens, then make the dressing. Put the minced shallot into a bowl and add the orange and lemon juices. Season well. Whisk together all the remaining ingredients for the dressing and add to the shallots.

Shuck the oysters and remove from their shells. Drain in a strainer set over a bowl. Just before serving, toss each oyster in seasoned flour, then beaten egg and bread crumbs. Melt a little clarified butter in a skillet and cook the oysters over medium heat until crisp and golden on all sides.

Meanwhile, toss the salad greens in a little dressing. Put a fistful of salad on each plate with four crisp sizzling oysters on top. Sprinkle with snipped parsley and serve immediately.

Mustard Greens

SERVES 6

I pound fresh spinach, minced
I pound mustard greens (just leaves
with their stems), minced
5 tablespoons coarsely chopped garlic
4–6 fresh hot green chile peppers
$1^1/_2$ –2 teaspoons salt
5–6 tablespoons fine cornmeal
3 tablespoons ghee, clarified butter, or
vegetable oil
$^3/_4$ cup minced onion
2-inch piece of fresh ginger, peeled
and cut into thin, long slivers
2 medium-sized, very ripe tomatoes,
finely chopped
A generous lump of unsalted butter

On Madhur Jaffrey's last visit to the school, she walked through the vegetable garden with me. She became excited when she spied our exuberant patch of mustard greens— cropping so well we could not use them fast enough. Her eyes sparkled as she told me about a wonderful Punjabi recipe she had found for mustard greens—the perfect way to use up some of our abundant crop. It was exquisite—worth growing mustard greens specially. The recipe comes from her book Flavors of India, *and I reprint with her kind permission.*

Combine the spinach, mustard greens, garlic, chiles, salt, and $3^1/_4$ cups water in a large, heavy pan. Set over high heat and bring to a boil. Cover, turn the heat to low, and simmer gently for $1^3/_4$ hours or until even the stems of the mustard green leaves have turned buttery soft. With the heat still on, add 5 tablespoons of the cornmeal, beating constantly with a whisk or a traditional greens masher as you do so. Using the same whisk or masher, mash the greens until they are fairly smooth (a little coarseness is desirable). The greens will thicken with the addition of the cornmeal. If they remain somewhat watery, add another tablespoon or so. Leave on very low heat.

Heat the ghee, clarified butter, or oil in a separate pan or wok over medium-high heat. When hot, put in the onion. Stir and fry until it turns golden brown. Add the ginger. Keep stirring and frying until the onion is medium-brown. Put in the tomatoes. Stir and fry until the tomatoes have softened and browned a little. Now pour this mixture over the greens and stir it in. Tip the greens into a serving dish, top with a lump of butter, and serve.

(RIGHT) *The potting shed, nestling in the corner here, was derelict when we arrived at Kinoith and had to be reglazed. I have had my eye on the Fernery, next door, as a project ripe for regeneration.*

Portobella Mushrooms with Parsley Pesto and Balsamic Vinegar

SERVES 6

6 Portobella mushrooms
Salt and freshly ground black pepper
2 large cloves garlic, minced
Olive oil
²/₃ cup diced cooked beets
5 tablespoons Homemade Chicken Stock
(see page 184) or Vegetable Stock
(see page 185)
2 tablespoons cream
5 tablespoons balsamic vinegar

Parsley or Basil Pesto (see page 186)

GARNISH
Fresh thyme leaves and edible flowers

If you cannot get Portobellas, use the biggest, fattest meaty mushrooms you can find. As a rule of thumb, mushrooms are often better when they are 4–5 days old, once they have had time to develop their flavor.

Preheat the oven to 475°F.

If you are using Portobella mushrooms, split them in half horizontally and arrange on a baking sheet in a single layer. Sprinkle with salt, a few grinds of pepper, and minced garlic. Drizzle with olive oil. Roast them in the preheated oven for 10–15 minutes or until cooked through.

Purée the beets with the chicken or vegetable stock and cream. Taste and correct the seasoning.

When the mushrooms are almost cooked, reduce the balsamic vinegar in a small saucepan until slightly syrupy. Sandwich the two pieces of each Portobella mushroom together with a dollop of Parsley or Basil Pesto. Arrange each one in the center of a hot plate. Drizzle balsamic vinegar and beet purée around the edge. Garnish with thyme leaves and edible flowers.

Spiced Eggplant with Goat Cheese and Arugula Leaves

SERVES 6

1³/₄ pounds eggplants
About 1 cup vegetable oil
(we use peanut)
1-inch cube fresh ginger, peeled and
coarsely chopped
6 large garlic cloves, peeled and
coarsely crushed
¹/₄ cup water
1 teaspoon fennel seeds
¹/₂ teaspoon cumin seeds
³/₄ pound very ripe tomatoes, peeled
and finely chopped, or a 14-ounce can
tomatoes plus 1 teaspoon sugar
1 tablespoon coriander seeds, freshly
ground
¹/₄ teaspoon ground turmeric
¹/₄ teaspoon cayenne pepper (more if
you like)
About 1 teaspoon salt

¹/₃ cup raisins
3 ounces soft goat cheese (we use
Ardsallagh or St. Tola)
¹/₂ cup heavy cream

GARNISH
Arugula leaves

Eggplant plants are quite beautiful and we always grow some in the conservatory. Make sure when you are buying or picking them that the top and the leaves are green and not brown and withered.

It is becoming more and more possible to buy many varieties of eggplant—at the farmers' markets in San Francisco or Berkeley, for instance, you will always find at least three organic varieties for sale. Indian eggplants would be good in this recipe, if you can find them. The spiced eggplant mixture is also good served cold or at room temperature as an accompaniment to cold lamb or pork.

Cut the eggplants into ³/₄ inch thick slices. You will need 12 slices (or 18 if you decide to do triple deckers). Heat ³/₄ cup oil in a deep 10- to 12-inch skillet. When hot, almost smoking, add a few eggplant slices and cook until golden and tender on both sides. Remove and drain on a wire rack over a baking sheet. Repeat with the remainder of the eggplant slices, adding more oil if necessary.

Put the ginger, garlic, and water into a blender or food processor. Blend until fairly smooth.

Heat the remaining oil in the skillet. When hot, add the fennel and cumin seeds. Stir for just a few seconds (be careful not to let them burn), then add the chopped tomatoes, the ginger-garlic mixture, coriander, turmeric, cayenne, and salt. Simmer, stirring occasionally, until the spice mixture thickens slightly, about 5–6 minutes.

Add the fried eggplant slices and the raisins, and mix gently with the spicy sauce. Cover the pan, reduce the heat to very low, and cook for 5–8 minutes.

Mix the goat cheese gently with the softly whipped cream. If the goat cheese is not soft and fresh like the Ardsallagh cheese we buy, it may be necessary to press it through a strainer before gently folding into the cream.

To serve: put one slice of spiced eggplant onto a warm plate and spoon a generous blob of goat cheese on top. Cover with another slice of eggplant and garnish with a few young arugula leaves and a little cracked pepper. Serve warm.

Crab Cakes with Cilantro Cream and Salsa Cruda

SERVES 5–6

I pound fresh crab meat
1¹/₂ cups soft white bread crumbs
2–3 teaspoons white wine vinegar
2 tablespoons ripe tomato chutney or
Ballymaloe Tomato Relish (it is now
available in many stores)
2 tablespoons softened butter
I teaspoon English mustard powder or
I heaping teaspoon Dijon mustard
2 tablespoons chopped fresh cilantro
A dash of Tabasco or a large pinch of
cayenne pepper
Salt and freshly ground black pepper
³/₄ cup Béchamel Sauce (see page 182)
Olive oil

COATING

All-purpose flour seasoned with salt
and pepper
I free-range egg white, beaten
White bread crumbs

Salsa Cruda (see page 187)

CILANTRO CREAM

3 tablespoons chopped fresh cilantro
³/₄ cup heavy cream, whipped
Sugar
Salt and freshly ground black pepper
I teaspoon freshly squeezed lemon juice

GARNISH

Fresh cilantro leaves

When I first arrived at Ballymaloe, it was a real treat to get crabs. The fishermen would always say that they could not be bothered to bring them in, as there was no call for them. We eventually started to say that we would buy the whole catch from them. This was risky, because they could bring in three or four, or they might bring in thirty to forty, in which case we would set about busily making crab salad, soups, and cakes. All around the table the family would be sitting bashing crab claws and salvaging all the beautiful meat. At the last moment my father-in-law, Ivan Allen, would enter the kitchen ceremoniously to "dress" the crab.

Nowadays crabs are landed regularly and, although the prices have rocketed, they are still very good value. These crab cakes are based on Ivan Allen's recipe.

Mix all the ingredients for the crab cakes, except the olive oil, in a bowl. Taste carefully and correct the seasoning—it should taste well seasoned and quite perky. Form the mixture into 10–12 cakes. Coat first with seasoned flour, then egg and finally bread crumbs. Put onto a baking sheet lined with parchment paper. Chill until firm.

Meanwhile, make the Cilantro Cream: Fold the chopped cilantro into the whipped cream, and add salt, freshly ground pepper, sugar, and the lemon juice. Taste and add a little more seasoning if necessary.

To serve: heat olive oil in a deep-fryer or in a skillet. Cook the crab cakes until crisp and golden. Drain on paper towels and serve immediately on hot plates with a dollop each of Cilantro Cream and some Salsa Cruda on the side.

Seared Tuna with Piperonata and Tapenade

SERVES 6

6 pieces of fresh tuna, 6 ounces each
2 tablespoons olive oil
Salt and freshly ground black pepper

Piperonata (see page 128)
Tapenade (see page 186)

GARNISH
6–8 sprigs fresh flat-leaf parsley or basil

Occasionally a tuna is caught off Ballycotton—great excitement! The secret of cooking tuna is to underdo it, like a rare steak, so that it is moist and juicy; well cooked it can become dry and dull. The sweetness of Piperonata and the gutsy taste of Tapenade are great with it.

First make the Piperonata and the Tapenade.

Preheat a ridged cast-iron grill pan. Brush the tuna with oil and season well with salt and pepper. Sear the tuna on the hot grill pan, turning it first in one direction and then the other, so that it develops a grid pattern from the ridges of the pan. Cook on both sides for 2–3 minutes. The center should still be "pink."

Meanwhile, reheat the Piperonata if necessary. Put a few tablespoons on each plate and place a piece of sizzling tuna on top. Put a little Tapenade on top or dot irregularly around the edge of the Piperonata. Add a few sprigs of flat-leaf parsley or basil and serve immediately.

Poached Striped Mullet with Hollandaise and Pea and Parsley Champ

SERVES 4

1 striped mullet, cleaned and scaled
Salt (see below)

Hollandaise Sauce (see page 182)

Pea and Parsley Champ (see page 126)

GARNISH
Segments of lemon
Fresh herbs, such as chervil, fennel, or flat-leaf parsley

Some people may feel, wrongly, that Hollandaise sauce is old hat, but our version, made without being reduced, with fine Irish butter, is completely exquisite. We serve it with poached fresh bass, salmon, or, in this case, striped mullet. The sauce turns this fish into an absolute feast. It is particularly delicious with soft and melting Pea and Parsley Champ.

Choose a saucepan that just fits the fish or, better still, use a small fish kettle. Measure in water carefully and add 1 heaping tablespoon of salt to every 5 cups water. Cover the saucepan or kettle and bring the water to a boil. Put in the fish, which should be just covered with water. Replace the lid on the saucepan, bring back to a boil, and simmer for 10 minutes only.

Meanwhile, make the Hollandaise Sauce.

Test the fish—it is cooked if the flesh comes away from the backbone close to the head when you lift it with the tip of a knife; if there is still resistance, replace the lid and leave the fish sitting in the water for a few more minutes.

To serve: put the fish on a hot serving dish and garnish with segments of lemon and fresh herbs. At the table lift off the skin and put a portion of fish onto each plate. Coat with the Hollandaise sauce and eat immediately with Pea and Parsley Champ. This fish is also lovely with Beurre Blanc (see page 29).

Warm Poached Mackerel with Bretonne Sauce

SERVES 4

4 very fresh mackerel
5 cups water
1 teaspoon salt

BRETONNE SAUCE
4 tablespoons butter, melted
2 egg yolks, preferably free-range
1 teaspoon Dijon mustard (we use Maille Verte aux Herbes)
$^1/_2$ teaspoon white wine vinegar
1 tablespoon chopped parsley or a mixture of chopped fresh chervil, chives, tarragon, and herb fennel

"The sun should never set on a mackerel," Tommy Sliney, the much-loved Ballycotton fish trader once told me, because within 5 hours the oil in the fish turns bitter. Really fresh mackerel, gently poached and served warm with this simple sauce, is an absolute feast and without question one of my favorite foods. Anyone who wonders why I get so excited about mackerel has not tasted it this way!

Cut the heads off the mackerel. Eviscerate and clean them, but keep whole. Bring the water to a boil and add the salt and the mackerel. Cover, bring back to boiling point, then remove from the heat. After about 5–8 minutes, check to see whether the fish are cooked. The flesh should lift off the bone. It will be tender and melting.

Meanwhile, make the sauce. Melt the butter and allow to boil. Put the egg yolks into a heatproof bowl. Add the mustard, wine vinegar, and herbs and mix well. Whisk the hot melted butter into the egg yolk mixture little by little, so that the sauce emulsifies. Keep warm by placing the heatproof bowl in a saucepan of hot but not boiling water.

When the mackerel is cool enough to handle, remove to a plate. Skin, lift the flesh carefully from the bones, and arrange on a serving dish. Coat with the sauce and serve while still warm, with a good green salad and new potatoes.

Roast Guinea Fowl with Parsnip Chips and Red-Currant Sauce

SERVES 4

I guinea fowl
A little softened or melted butter

Homemade Game or Chicken Stock (see page 184)

STUFFING
3 tablespoons butter
$1/2$ cup chopped onions
I cup bread crumbs
I tablespoon chopped fresh herbs, such as parsley, thyme, chives, and marjoram
Salt and freshly ground black pepper

Parsnip Chips (see page 127)
Red-Currant Sauce (see page 187)

GARNISH
Sprigs of watercress

James Veale rears plump guinea fowl for us, which have a superb flavor. We used to keep guinea fowls ourselves, but the "gebak, gebak, gebak" noise that they make frightened my chickens, and Frank complained that they had been put off laying. One night the guinea fowl all disappeared—I didn't ask what happened to them…

Preheat the oven to 375°F.

To make the stuffing, melt the butter and sweat the onions until soft but not colored, then remove from the heat. Stir in the soft white bread crumbs and freshly chopped herbs, season with salt and pepper, and taste. Unless you are going to cook the bird right away, let the stuffing become quite cold before putting it into the bird.

Season the cavity with salt and pepper and stuff the guinea fowl loosely. Smear the breast and legs with softened or melted butter. Roast in the preheated oven for about $1^{1}/_{4}$ hours. Test by pricking the leg at the thickest point: the juices should run clear.

Meanwhile, make the Red-Currant Sauce and the Parsnip Chips.

Spoon off any surplus fat from the roasting pan (keep it for roasting or sautéing potatoes). Deglaze the pan with game or chicken stock. Bring to a boil and use a whisk to dislodge the crusty caramelized juices so they can dissolve into the gravy. Season with salt and pepper, taste, and boil until you are happy with the flavor. Pour into a hot sauce-boat.

Carve the guinea fowl into four portions, giving each person some brown and some white meat. Spoon a little gravy over the meat. Pile some Parsnip Chips over the top. Garnish with large sprigs of watercress and serve with Red-Currant Sauce.

119

Chargrilled Sirloin Steak with Salsa Verde and Rustic Roast Potatoes

SERVES 2

2 sirloin steaks, 6 ounces each, or
1 rib steak, cut 2 inches thick
1 clove of garlic

Salsa Verde (see page 187)

RUSTIC ROAST POTATOES
2 pounds small new potatoes
Extra virgin olive oil
Freshly ground black pepper

SALAD AND DRESSING
2 bunches arugula, watercress, or mixed lettuces
1 tablespoon red wine vinegar
3 tablespoons extra virgin olive oil
Sea salt and freshly ground black pepper

This was cooked for me by my great friend Mary Risley, who owns the highly acclaimed Tante Marie Cooking School in San Francisco. Chargrilled steak has a wonderful flavor, but an iron grill pan also gives a delicious result.

Preheat the oven to 435°F.

Wash the potatoes and rub with olive oil. Sprinkle with salt and freshly ground pepper. Put the potatoes onto a baking sheet and roast in the preheated oven until crisp and tender—about 35 minutes.

To prepare the steak, rub both sides with a cut clove of garlic, drizzle with extra virgin olive oil, and sprinkle with pepper. Leave at room temperature for at least 30 minutes.

Meanwhile, make the Salsa Verde.

At the last minute, salt the steak on both sides and grill over a charcoal fire or on a grill pan, then let relax for 5 minutes on a wooden board.

Put the arugula leaves, watercress sprigs, or salad lettuce into a bowl. Mix the red wine vinegar with the extra virgin olive oil. Season well with salt and pepper. Toss the salad in a little dressing, just enough to make the leaves glisten. Arrange on a serving plate. Pop the roast potatoes around the sides. Slice the steak thickly at an angle. Arrange the slices of steak on the salad and drizzle the Salsa Verde over the meat.

Roast Pork with Spiced Eggplant

I despair of the flavor of intensively reared animals, quite apart from my unease over their welfare. We rear our own or get our meat from Seamus Hogan, a poet and farmer from Kanturk, County Cork, or our neighbor Patty Walsh. Their pork is so juicy it has you licking your fingers. We like our pork with the skin, or rind, left on, and if you can find a butcher who will prepare the roast for you this way, treasure him.

SERVES 10–12

A 5-pound loin of pork, preferably with
the rind intact
Salt and freshly ground black pepper
2 tablespoons chopped mixed fresh herbs
(such as parsley, thyme, chives,
marjoram, savory, and perhaps a little
sage or rosemary)

Spiced Eggplant mixture (see page 112)
(use up to twice the amount in the
recipe, depending on your appetite)

Puy Lentils (see page 131)

Preheat the oven to 375°F.

Score the rind at ¼-inch intervals, running with the grain—ask your
butcher to do this if possible, because the rind, particularly of free-range
pork, can be quite tough. This is to give you what we call crackling, and to
make it easier to carve the roast later.

Put the pork, skin-side down, on a chopping board, season with salt and
pepper, and sprinkle with freshly chopped herbs. Roll up tightly and tie
with cotton string. Sprinkle some salt over the rind. Roast on a rack in a
roasting pan in the preheated oven, allowing 25–28 minutes for each pound.
Baste with the rendered pork fat every now and then.

Meanwhile, cook the Spiced Eggplant and Puy Lentils.

Just before the end of the cooking time, transfer the pork to another
roasting pan. Return the meat to the oven and increase the temperature to
450°F to crisp the crackling further.

When the pork is cooked, the juices will run clear and a meat thermometer
should register an internal temperature of at least 170°F. Put the pork onto
a hot carving dish and let rest for 10–15 minutes in a low oven before
carving. Serve with the Spiced Eggplant and the Puy Lentils. Roast potatoes
and a green salad would also make a good accompaniment.

Glazed Ham with Tomato Fondue and Scallion Champ

SERVES 12–15

A 4- to 5-pound boneless, uncooked country-cured ham, either smoked or unsmoked, with a nice layer of fat
About 20–30 whole cloves
1$^3/_4$ cups light brown sugar
3–4 tablespoons pineapple juice

Tomato Fondue (see page 182)

Scallion Champ (see page 40)

Irish ham and bacon have quite a different flavor from that of other countries. When you can buy a cured loin from an Irish bacon pig with a nice layer of fat it has a sweet, juicy flavor. Yet so strong is the predominant dietary fear that most consumers ask for meat with no fat at all! This makes no sense, either from the culinary or the health angle, and I lose sleep trying to work out how to get this simple message across, now that people have been led to believe that fat is public enemy number one!

The ham should be cooked with the rind on to keep in the flavor. Cured pork is one of the traditional flavors of Ireland that we serve with pride to our guests.

Cover the ham with cold water and bring slowly to a boil. If the ham is very salty, a white froth forms on top of the water, in which case it is best to discard the water. It may be necessary to change the water several times, depending on how salty the ham is. Finally, cover it with hot water and simmer until almost cooked, allowing about 20 minutes to each pound.

Preheat the oven to 475°F.

Remove the rind carefully—it will peel off in a sheet. Score the fat in a diamond pattern and stud with cloves. Mix the brown sugar to a thick paste with a little pineapple juice—be careful not to make it too liquid. Spread this paste over the fat. Put into a roasting pan just large enough to fit the ham.

Bake in the preheated oven for 20–30 minutes or until the top of the ham has caramelized. Spoon the glaze up over the ham several times during this baking and keep an eye on it. At first nothing much happens, but once the glaze heats up it can caramelize very quickly and within minutes turn black and acrid—believe me, I know from experience!

Serve with Tomato Fondue and Scallion Champ.

Tarragon Chicken with Chile and Tomato Fondue

SERVES 4–6

A 3¹/₄-pound chicken (free-range if possible)
Salt and freshly ground black pepper
2 tablespoons chopped fresh French tarragon, plus sprig of tarragon
1¹/₂ tablespoons butter
²/₃ cup Homemade Chicken Stock (optional) (see page 184)
²/₃ cup heavy cream
Roux (optional) (see page 182)

Chile and Tomato Fondue (see page 130)

GARNISH
Sprigs of fresh tarragon

Chicken with tarragon is a great classic, and this method of cooking chicken inside a casserole preserves the juices. It is also a splendid way to cook pheasant, turkey, and guinea fowl. Vary the herbs—marjoram is good, too.

Preheat the oven to 350°F.

Remove the wing tips and wishbone from the chicken and keep for making stock. Season the cavity of the chicken with salt and pepper. Stuff a sprig of tarragon inside—this will perfume the chicken flesh as it cooks. Mix 1 tablespoon chopped tarragon with two-thirds of the butter. Smear the remaining butter over the breast of the chicken. An oval flameproof casserole of 2¹/₂-quart capacity, is the perfect size for the recipe.

Place the chicken, breast-side down, in the casserole and let it brown over a gentle heat. This may take up to 6–7 minutes—don't hurry it or you may burn the bottom of the casserole and spoil the flavor of the sauce later. Turn the chicken breast-side up and smear the tarragon butter over the breast and legs. Season with salt and pepper. Cover the casserole and put into the preheated oven to cook for 1¹/₄–1¹/₂ hours. To test if the chicken is cooked, pierce the flesh between the breast and thigh. This is the last place to cook, so if there is no trace of pink here and if the juices are clear, the chicken is certainly cooked. (The internal temperature should be at least 170°F.)

Meanwhile, make the Chile and Tomato Fondue.

Remove the chicken to a carving dish and let it rest while you make the sauce. Spoon every scrap of fat from the juices and add the stock, cream, and remaining chopped tarragon. Boil until the sauce thickens slightly.

Alternatively, bring the liquid to a boil, and whisk in just enough Roux to thicken the sauce to a light coating consistency. Taste and add the chopped tarragon and a little more seasoning if necessary. If the sauce is thickened with Roux, this dish can be reheated.

Carve the chicken into 4–6 portions; each person should have some white and some dark meat. Arrange on a serving dish, coat with the sauce, and serve immediately with the Chile and Tomato Fondue.

Hamburgers with Ginger Mushrooms and Buffalo Fries

SERVES 4–6

I tablespoon butter
$^1/_2$ cup chopped onion
I pound ground round
$^1/_2$ teaspoon fresh thyme leaves
$^1/_2$ teaspoon minced parsley
I egg, preferably free-range, beaten
Salt and freshly ground black pepper
Pork caul fat (optional)
Oil for frying

Ginger Mushrooms (see page 130)

BUFFALO FRIES
6 large potatoes, unpeeled
Oil for deep-frying—olive or a mixture
of olive and sunflower
Salt

Dressed green salad, cherry tomatoes,
and scallions (optional)

This scrummy combination is one of Timmy's specialties, adored and much requested by the children, their friends, and me too!.

First make the hamburgers. Melt the butter in a saucepan, toss in the chopped onion, and sweat until soft but not colored; then leave to get cold. Mix the ground beef with the herbs and beaten egg. Season with salt and pepper, add the onion, and mix well. Fry a tiny bit in the pan, taste to check the seasoning, and adjust if necessary. Then shape into hamburgers, 4–6 depending on the size you require. Wrap each one loosely in caul fat, if using. Keep refrigerated.

Next make the Ginger Mushrooms and keep aside.

Scrub the potatoes and cut into wedges from top to bottom—they should be about $^3/_4$ inch thick and at least $2^1/_2$ inches long. If you like, rinse the potatoes quickly in cold water, but do not soak; dry them meticulously with a dish towel or paper towels before cooking. Heat the oil in the deep-fryer to 350°F. Fry the potatoes for 5–8 minutes, depending on size, then drain.

Next, fry the hamburgers and reheat the Ginger Mushrooms. Increase the temperature of the oil to 425°F and cook the Buffalo Fries again, for I–2 minutes, until crisp and golden. Drain the fries well on paper towels and sprinkle with salt.

To serve: put the hamburgers onto hot plates, spoon some Ginger Mushrooms over the side of the hamburgers, and pile on the crisp Buffalo Fries. Put a little green salad tossed in a well-flavored dressing on the side, with one or two cherry tomatoes and a perky scallion. Serve immediately and tuck in.

Aileen's Pappardelle with Roasted Pumpkin, Pine Nuts, and Arugula Leaves

A gorgeous autumn pasta dish conjured up by Aileen Murphy, one of the bright young chefs in the Ballymaloe kitchen. We use the basic idea of the recipe in many ways during the rest of the year, adding everything from arugula, roasted yellow sweet peppers, and pine nuts to arugula, fava beans, and a sprinkling of Parmesan.

SERVES 4

A ¹/₂-pound piece of pumpkin
Salt and freshly ground black pepper
Melted butter
2 heaping tablespoons pine nuts
1 cup heavy cream
3 tablespoons butter
10 tablespoons freshly grated Parmesan cheese (Parmigiano Reggiano is best)
Grating of nutmeg
1 pound fresh pappardelle
16–24 arugula leaves, depending on size —ours are often quite big—reserving a few as a garnish
Extra Parmesan cheese

Preheat the oven to 350°F.

Season the pumpkin with salt and pepper. Drizzle with melted butter, cover loosely with aluminum foil, and roast in the preheated oven for 25 minutes or until the pumpkin is tender. Cut into 1-inch cubes and keep warm. Toast the pine nuts until golden, either in the oven or under the broiler.

Put the cream and butter in a saucepan and simmer over medium heat for less than a minute, by which time the butter and cream will have slightly thickened. Add the Parmesan, salt, pepper, and a grating of nutmeg. Remove from the heat and set aside for a few minutes until required.

Bring a large pot of water to a boil, add 2 tablespoons salt, and cook the pasta for 2–3 minutes. Drain.

While the pasta is cooking, reheat the sauce gently and add the cubed pumpkin and the toasted pine nuts.

Drain the pasta and toss gently in the sauce. Taste and correct the seasoning. Finally, add most of the arugula leaves and allow to wilt slightly. Serve immediately in preheated pasta dishes. Sprinkle with extra Parmesan cheese and the rest of the fresh arugula leaves as a garnish.

Leek Champ

SERVES 4–6

6–8 potatoes suitable for mashing
4 medium-sized leeks
7 tablespoons butter
Salt and freshly ground black pepper
I tablespoon water, if necessary
$1^1/_4$–$1^1/_2$ cups milk
I tablespoon chopped fresh chives

I have converted many people who cannot bear boiled leeks with this delicious dish. I found it when I was researching my Irish Traditional Food *book. It is one of many versions of champ and comes from Ulster.*

Scrub the potatoes. Cover with cold water and boil them in their skins. Halfway through cooking, pour off half the water, cover the pan, and steam until fully cooked.

Cut off the dark green leaves from the top of the leeks (wash and add to the stock-pot or use for making green leek soup). Slit the leeks about halfway down the center and wash well under cold running water. Slice into $^1/_4$-inch rounds. Melt 3 tablespoons of the butter in a heavy saucepan; when it foams, add the sliced leeks and toss gently to coat with butter. Season with salt and pepper and add the water if necessary. Cover with a circle of parchment paper and a close-fitting lid. Reduce the heat and cook very gently for 10–15 minutes, or until soft, tender, and juicy. Check and stir every now and then during cooking.

Bring the milk to a boil with the chives and simmer for 3–4 minutes; remove from heat and let infuse. Peel the freshly boiled potatoes, mash them, and, while hot, mix with the boiling milk and chives. Add the drained leeks and beat in the remaining butter. Season to taste with salt and pepper. The champ should be soft and melting.

Leek Champ may be put aside and reheated later in a preheated oven at 350°F. Cover with aluminum foil while it reheats so that it does not get a skin over the top.

Pea and Parsley Champ

SERVES 4

2 pounds potatoes suitable for mashing
Salt and freshly ground black pepper
$1^1/_4$ cups milk
$1^1/_2$ cups shelled fresh young peas
$^1/_2$ cup chopped parsley
2–4 tablespoons butter (traditionally, strong country butter would have been used)

Another version of the traditional Irish champ—again from Ulster.

Scrub the potatoes. Put into a saucepan and cook in their skins in boiling salted water until tender. Drain thoroughly and dry over the heat in the saucepan for a few minutes. Mash the potatoes while hot.

Meanwhile, bring the milk to a boil and add the peas. Simmer until the peas are just cooked—allow about 8–10 minutes. Drop in the chopped parsley for the final 2 minutes of cooking. Add the hot milk mixture to the potatoes. Season well. Add butter to taste and beat until light and fluffy. The texture should be soft and moist. Serve hot.

Parsnip Chips

SERVES 6–8

I large parsnip (other root vegetables can
also be used)
Sunflower or peanut oil
Salt

*We serve these delicious chips on warm salads, as a garnish for roast pheasant or
guinea fowl, and as a topping for parsnip or other root vegetable soup. Delicious chips
can be made from other vegetables, apart from the much-loved potato; celery root, beet,
leek, and even carrots are also good. The drier the slices, the better.*

Peel the parsnip. Either slice into wafer-thin rounds or peel off long slivers
lengthwise with a swivel-top peeler. Let dry for I hour.

Heat good-quality oil in a deep-fryer to 400°F. Drop a few chips at a time
into the hot oil; they color and crisp up very quickly. Drain on paper towels
and sprinkle lightly with salt.

Pattypan Squash with
Basil or Marjoram

SERVES 6

12–18 little pattypan squash or a
mixture of pattypan squash
and small zucchini
Olive oil
Salt and freshly ground black pepper
2 tablespoons torn fresh basil leaves or
chopped marjoram
A few drops of lemon juice (optional)

*When I first grew pattypan squash in the vegetable garden, I waited eagerly for them
to crop. I tasted, full of anticipation, but, sadly, they are disappointing from the
flavor angle. Nonetheless, they look adorable, have beautiful blossoms, and take on
other flavors readily. Also, the more you pick, the more they come! They are great with
Chile and Tomato Fondue (see page 130).*

Trim the pattypan squash and cut each one into six or eight pie-shaped
pieces, depending on size. Cut the zucchini, if using, on the diagonal into
$1/3$-inch slices.

Heat a few tablespoons of olive oil in a heavy skillet or wok and add the
squash. Season with salt and pepper and toss rapidly over the heat. Add
the torn or chopped herbs and toss for another minute or so. Taste and
correct the seasoning—a few drops of lemon juice might be good. Serve
immediately.

Fresh Corn with Marjoram

SERVES 6

6 ears of corn, preferably freshly picked
Salt and freshly ground black pepper
2–4 tablespoons butter
1–2 tablespoons chopped fresh
annual marjoram

This is Timmy's combination, and the freshest corn is essential. We are lucky because we can pick ours in the garden and rush it to the kitchen.

Bring a large saucepan of water to a boil. Meanwhile, shuck the corn and trim both ends. When the water is boiling, add some salt and the corn. Cover the saucepan and bring back to a boil; cook for just 3 minutes.

Drain the corn and let cool, then slice the kernels off each cob. Melt a little butter in a saucepan. Add the corn and season with salt and pepper. Add the marjoram and stir once or twice. Taste and correct the seasoning. Serve immediately.

Piperonata

SERVES 8–10

2 tablespoons extra virgin olive oil
1 onion, sliced
1 clove garlic, minced
2 red sweet peppers
2 green sweet peppers
6 large, very ripe tomatoes
Salt and freshly ground black pepper
Sugar
A few leaves of fresh basil

This is one of the indispensable trio of vegetable stews that we always have on hand. We use it not only as a vegetable, but also as a topping for pizzas, as a sauce for pasta, grilled fish, or meat, and as a filling for omelettes and crêpes. You can vary the herbs or add some hot chile pepper.

Heat the olive oil in a flameproof casserole. Add the sliced onion, stir, and cook for a few seconds. Add the garlic. Cover and let soften over a gentle heat while the peppers are being prepared.

Halve the peppers and remove the seeds. Cut into quarters and then into strips across rather than lengthwise. The onion should be soft and tender by now, so add the peppers and toss well; replace the lid and continue to cook.

Meanwhile, peel the tomatoes (scald in boiling water for 10 seconds, pour off the water, and peel immediately). Slice the tomatoes and add to the casserole. Season with salt, pepper, sugar, and a few leaves of fresh basil. Cook gently until the vegetables are just soft—about 30 minutes.

Stir-Fried Zucchini with Garlic and Ginger

We grow lots and lots of zucchini, and we need endless recipes to use them up. We often toss zucchini prepared like this into pasta and tear in some blossom at the last minute.

SERVES 6

1 1/2 pounds small zucchini, each about
6 inches long
Salt
3 tablespoons olive oil
2 cloves garlic, minced
1 tablespoon grated fresh ginger root
Lots of freshly ground black pepper

Trim the zucchini. Cut crosswise into 1/4-inch slices. If the zucchini are large, cut each in half lengthwise and, using a teaspoon or small melon baller, scrape away all the seeds. Then cut the zucchini crosswise into 1/4-inch slices. Put in a bowl or colander, sprinkle lightly with salt, and mix well. Set aside for 20 minutes. Drain and pat dry.

Heat a wok or heavy skillet over high heat. When it is hot, pour in the oil. Add the garlic and ginger. Stir once or twice, then put in the zucchini immediately. Continue to toss over the heat for 3–4 minutes. The zucchini should not be allowed to get limp. Add freshly ground black pepper, taste, and serve immediately.

Ginger Mushrooms

SERVES 6

1–2 tablespoons butter
$^1/_2$ cup minced onion
3 cups sliced mushrooms
Salt and freshly ground black pepper
A squeeze of lemon juice
$^1/_2$ cup heavy cream
I teaspoon freshly grated ginger
3 tablespoons slivered almonds,
lightly toasted
$^1/_2$ tablespoon chopped parsley
$^1/_2$ tablespoon chopped fresh chives

Melt the butter in a heavy saucepan until it foams. Add the minced onions, cover, and sweat on low heat for 5–6 minutes or until quite soft but not colored. Meanwhile, cook the mushrooms in a hot skillet, in batches if necessary. Season each batch with salt, pepper, and a tiny squeeze of lemon juice. Add the mushrooms to the onions in the saucepan, then add the cream, ginger, and almonds. Let bubble for a few minutes. Taste and correct the seasoning, and add the parsley and chives.

Timmy's Chile and Tomato Fondue

SERVES 4–6

$^3/_4$ cup sliced onions
I clove garlic, minced
2 teaspoons olive oil
4 large Hungarian Wax chile peppers
I pound very ripe tomatoes, peeled and
sliced (or, in winter, use canned)
Salt, freshly ground pepper, and sugar
Chopped fresh herbs, such as thyme,
parsley, annual marjoram, and cilantro

Hungarian Wax chile peppers, the variety Timmy uses for his Chile and Tomato Fondue, are about 5 inches long—sweet and not too hot. Leave the seeds in for extra kick.

Sweat the sliced onions and the garlic in the olive oil over low heat for about 10 minutes. Add the sliced chiles and continue to sweat until soft. It is vital for the success of this dish that the onions are completely soft before the tomatoes are added. Stir in the tomatoes. Season with salt, pepper, and sugar and add a generous sprinkling of chopped herbs. Cook for 10–20 more minutes or until the tomato softens. Add lots of chopped cilantro just before serving.

Pink Fir Apple Potatoes

SERVES 2–4

I pound Pink Fir Apple potatoes
Maldon sea salt
Butter

This is one of the many old potato varieties that we grow every year in the garden. Pink Fir Apple potatoes are waxy in texture, so are good for potato salad. Other similar varieties of potato, such as Yukon Gold, Yellow Finn, and fingerlings, are delicious this way, too.

Scrub the potatoes thoroughly. Boil in well-salted water until cooked through—about 15–20 minutes. Serve immediately with sea salt and lots of butter. We sometimes cut them lengthwise and toss them in butter or extra virgin olive oil and sea salt before serving.

Puy Lentils

SERVES 4–6

1 heaping cup Puy lentils
1 carrot
1 onion, spiked with 2 cloves
Bouquet of herbs
Butter or extra virgin olive oil
Lots of freshly squeezed lemon juice
About 2 tablespoons chopped
fresh herbs (such as oregano,
annual marjoram, or parsley)
Sea salt and freshly ground black pepper

Green-speckled lentilles du Puy *are the aristocrats of the lentil family. They cook in minutes and can play a starring or supporting role in many meals.*

Rinse the lentils and put into a large saucepan. Cover with cold water and add the carrot, onion, and bouquet garni. Bring slowly to a boil, then reduce the heat and simmer very gently for 10–15 minutes, testing regularly. The lentils should be *al dente* but not hard. Drain, and remove and discard the carrot, onion, and bouquet garni. Toss the lentils while warm with a large lump of butter or some extra virgin olive oil, then add lots of freshly squeezed lemon juice and some freshly chopped herbs. Season with sea salt and freshly ground black pepper. Serve immediately.

Note: Lentils are also good with a little minced hot chile pepper added. Add the quantity you like—say half a small chile with the seeds removed.

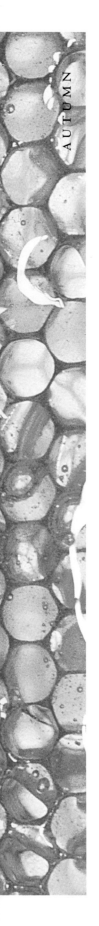

Autumn Leaves with Chocolate Mousse

SERVES 8–10

CHOCOLATE MOUSSE
3 ounces best quality bittersweet
chocolate
1 ounce unsweetened chocolate
3 tablespoons dark rum
1 envelope unflavored gelatin
5 eggs, preferably free-range
6 tablespoons sugar
1¹/₂ cups heavy cream, softly whipped

CHOCOLATE LEAVES
White chocolate
Semisweet chocolate
Milk chocolate
Interestingly shaped leaves, such as
maple and rose
Softly whipped cream

DECORATION
Confectioners' sugar
Unsweetened cocoa powder

I first ate something like this at the Clarence Hotel in Dublin, in the "tearooms." I thought that it was such a fun idea that I recreated it later at home. Choose large, well-veined leaves and a good chocolate that has a high percentage of cocoa butter (avoid chocolate made with vegetable fat, as it tastes inferior). We use the Lesmé, Callebaut, and Valrhona brands.

First make the chocolate mousse. Put the bittersweet and unsweetened chocolates, rum, and 1 tablespoon water in a saucepan and melt over low heat. Put the gelatin in a small heatproof bowl with 2 tablespoons water and let soften, then dissolve over a saucepan of boiling water. Beat three whole eggs and two yolks with the sugar to a stiff mousse. Add a few tablespoons of this mixture to the gelatin, stir well, and then mix with the rest.

Beat the two remaining egg whites stiffly. Fold the chocolate into the mousse, followed quickly by the softly whipped cream and stiffly beaten egg white. The mousse sets very quickly once the chocolate is mixed with the gelatin, so speed is of the essence. Put into individual molds to set or pour into a shallow dish so it can be scooped out later. Chill the mousse for several hours.

To make the leaves, melt the white, semisweet, and milk chocolates gently in separate heatproof bowls in a very low oven or over simmering water. Paint the chocolate over the undersides of the leaves using the back of a teaspoon or a flat pastry brush. Be careful not to let the chocolate dribble over the edges, otherwise the leaves will be difficult to peel off later. Let set on parchment paper in a cool place. Make a mixture of colors, shapes, and sizes. When the chocolate is set and firm, peel the leaves off carefully. If you are in a hurry, you can speed up the setting process by putting the leaves into the refrigerator, but this does dull the chocolate somewhat.

To assemble: put one unmolded chocolate mousse or a scoop of the mixture onto a chilled white plate. Decorate with overlapping chocolate leaves, and sprinkle with a little confectioners' sugar and unsweetened cocoa powder. Serve immediately.

Yogurt with Apple-Blossom Honey and Toasted Hazelnuts

PER PERSON

About I heaping tablespoon sweet-tasting hazelnuts
Plain yogurt, or a goat milk yogurt
About 2 tablespoons apple-blossom honey or strongly flavored honey

We have just two beehives down at the end of the apple orchard. Some years, if the weather is inclement, we get very few sections, but in 1996 my bees produced "twice the national average." I was pleased as Punch. Although the orchard is five acres of mixed Worcester Pearmain, Bramley's Seedling, and Grenadier, I don't suppose the honey is totally from the apple blossom, but it must be predominantly so. In any case, it tastes wonderful. In autumn we are fortunate to be able to gather our own hazelnuts from the nut walk planted by Lydia Strangman at the beginning of the twentieth century.

We use a superb sheep's milk yogurt made by Oliver Jungwirth on Manch Farm in West Cork, from the milk of their organically reared Friesland sheep. It comes in dark glass jars to preserve the vitamins and minerals—more expensive than other yogurt, but worth every penny.

Preheat the oven to 400°F.

Put the hazelnuts onto a baking sheet and bake in the preheated oven for 8–10 minutes or until the skins loosen. Remove from the oven and, as soon as they are cool enough to handle, rub off the thin papery skins. (I usually put them into a dish towel, gather up the edges like a pouch, rub the towel against the nuts for a minute or so, and, hey presto, virtually all the skins come off in one go.) If the nuts are still very pale, put them back into the oven for a few more minutes until pale golden and crisp. Chop coarsely.

Just before serving, spoon a generous portion of chilled yogurt onto a cold plate, drizzle generously with really good honey, and sprinkle with the toasted hazelnuts. Eat immediately.

Baked Crimson Bramleys with Brown Sugar and Cream

SERVES 6

6 Crimson Bramley apples, or other large apples suitable for baking
About 6 heaping tablespoons granulated sugar
6 tablespoons butter

Softly whipped cream
Brown sugar

Granpoppy, my maternal grandfather, loved his food. He kept ducks, geese, and chickens for the table. The orchard contained many old varieties of apple, and one I particularly remember was a Crimson Bramley, sometimes made into tarts by my grandmother or served as a fluffy applesauce with roast duck or goose. Granpoppy's favorite, though, was baked apples, which he ate almost every evening throughout the autumn. We have just one tree of Crimson Bramleys; some seasons the apples color to a rich crimson and other years they are paler. I have never discovered why.

Preheat the oven to 400°F.

Core the apples cleanly and score the skin around the "equator." Put the apples side by side in a baking dish. Fill the centers with a generous tablespoon of sugar and put a generous dab of butter on top. Pour a little water into the bottom of the dish—about ¹/₄ inch will be enough. Cover with a sheet of wax paper.

Bake in the preheated oven for about 45 minutes. The cooking time will depend on the size of the apples. They are ready to eat when they are soft and bursting out of their skins.

Genteel people sometimes feel they ought not to allow the apples to burst, but they are immeasurably better when they do. Serve immediately, as they soon collapse and look sad and wizened. Softly whipped cream and a generous sprinkling of brown sugar complete the feast.

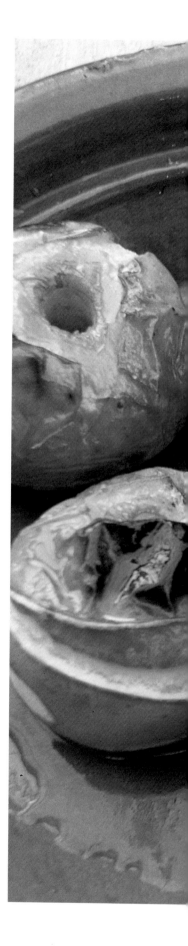

MAKES 9–10

SYRUP
1 cup plus 2 tablespoons sugar
1 cup water
4 sprigs fresh mint
2 teaspoons framboise (raspberry eau-de-vie)
1 tablespoon freshly squeezed lemon juice

3 heaping teaspoons unflavored gelatin
4 cups fresh autumn raspberries

MINT CREAM
About 15 fresh mint leaves
1 tablespoon lemon juice
²/₃ cup heavy cream

DECORATION
Fresh mint leaves
Rapberries

YOU WILL NEED
9–10 round molds—3 fluid ounce capacity, 2¹/₂ inches inside diameter, 1¹/₄ inches deep

Autumn Raspberry Gelatins with Fresh Mint Cream

We use our Heritage variety of autumn raspberry, which bears fruit until December. They are slow to ripen but this means their flavor is more intense, and we really value their long season. These fresh-tasting gelatins are the perfect finale to a rich meal.

Prepare the syrup by bringing the sugar, water, and mint leaves to a boil slowly. Simmer for a few minutes. Let cool, then add the framboise and lemon juice.

Brush the inside of the molds with non-scented oil. I use light peanut or sunflower oil.

Soften the gelatin in 3 tablespoons water, then set the bowl in a pan of simmering water until the gelatin has completely dissolved.

Remove the mint leaves from the syrup, then pour the syrup onto the gelatin. Mix well. Add the raspberries and stir gently. Spoon immediately into the oiled molds, smoothing over the top so they will not be wobbly when you later unmold them onto a plate. Put them into the refrigerator and let set for 3–4 hours or overnight.

Meanwhile, make the Mint Cream. Crush the mint leaves to a paste in a mortar and pestle with the lemon juice. Add the cream and stir—the lemon juice will thicken the cream. If the cream becomes too thick, add a little water.

To serve: spread a little Mint Cream on a chilled plate, unmold a raspberry gelatin, and place in the center. Arrange five mint leaves on the mint cream around the gelatin and decorate with a few perfect raspberries. Repeat with the other gelatins. Serve chilled.

Poached Plums with Mascarpone Cheese

SERVES 4

2 cups sugar
2 cups water
2 pounds fresh plums
Mascarpone cheese
Extra sugar to taste

Poach the plums whole—they will taste better, but quite apart from that you will have the fun of playing "He loves me—he loves me not!" You could just fix it by making sure you take an uneven number! The poached plums keep very well in the refrigerator and are delicious for breakfast—without the mascarpone.

Put the sugar and water into a saucepan and bring to a boil slowly. Tip in the plums, cover the saucepan, and poach until they begin to burst. Turn into a bowl and serve warm with some sweetened mascarpone cheese melting over the top. Divine.

Julia Wight's Quince Paste

Quinces
Sugar

YOU WILL NEED
2 baking pans, measuring about
9 by 12 inches

Quince is the most beautiful fruit and so wonderfully fragrant. If you bring a bowlful into the kitchen, they will perfume the whole house. By the time I can finally bear to cook my quinces they are often too old to use. My friend Julia Wight, whose food I adore, makes this quince paste every year and her friends vie for her affections in order to secure a gift of it!

This paste is absolutely delicious served with a spoonful of soft goat cheese and a leaf of sweet cicely or rose geranium. Julia also loves quince paste with Stilton or Cashel Blue cheese.

Preheat the oven to 200°F.

With a cloth rub the down off the skins of as many quinces as you can pack into a large earthenware jar. Do not add any water. Cover the jar and place in a low oven for about 4 hours or until the fruit is easily pierced with a skewer. Quarter the fruit, remove the core and blemishes, and put through a food mill, using the biggest disk. (If you do not have one, buy one!)

Weigh the pulp, and add ³/₄ pound (I³/₄ cups) of sugar to every pound of pulp. Cook in a preserving kettle over medium heat, stirring continuously with a wooden spatula, until the mixture is rich colored and it stops running together again when the spatula is drawn through.

Line the pans with parchment paper, fill with the paste, and leave overnight to get quite cold.

The following day, dry out the pans of paste in a low oven (200°F) for about 4 hours or until quite firm. Check the paste is ready by lifting a corner; it should be solid all the way through. When the paste has cooled, cut in four strips, wrap in parchment, and store in an airtight container. It will keep for about 4 months, but is best eaten when freshly made, cut into I-inch squares, as a sweetmeat.

Sloe or Damson Gin

Sloes are very tart, tiny purple plums. They grow on prickly bushes on the top of stone walls and are also found in the hedgerows around our farm. They are in season in September and October. Damson plums, also autumn fruits, are less tart and plump than sloes and can be interchanged in this recipe.

MAKES 6 1/2 CUPS

MAKES 6 1/2 CUPS

3 cups sloes or damsons
1 3/4 cups white sugar
5 cups gin or poteen

On our 12-week course we take the students out to pick damsons and sloes. They are always disappointed that the sloe gin is only made as a demonstration! I make a lot of sloe gin and give it away as Christmas presents. It is lethal, as it slips down so easily! You can also sweeten it and freeze it as a granita.

Wash and dry the sloes or damsons. Prick each one in several places—we use a clean darning needle. It sounds tedious, but can be enjoyable if you make yourself a cup of coffee, psyche yourself up, and turn your thoughts to Christmas, by which time your sloe or damson gin will taste wonderful and make great gifts.

Put the prepared fruit into a sterilized canning jar. Cover with the sugar and gin and seal tightly. Shake the jar every other day to start with, and then every now and then for 3–4 months, by which time the gin will be ready to strain and bottle. It will improve with keeping, so try to resist drinking it for another few months.

Winter

The shell house looks stunning with the thin winter light filtering through the diamond-shaped panes of the Gothic windows. Timmy fought long and hard to dissuade me from this folly, but, in the end, it was built and now he adores it.

Perhaps it is because I was reared far from the sea that I have always been enchanted by sea shells. I'd been collecting them in a haphazard way for years and they were piling up everywhere. I'd seen an article in an old gardening books about a shell grotto, mysterious and fantastical, and I immediately wanted to create something similar.

Timmy lives in fear of my next crazy idea and, as the shells piled up, he knew I would eventually build it. "Fate is great"— by sheer

(LEFT AND ABOVE) *The octagonal shellhouse, at the end of the herbacious borders, is a memorable feature adjacent to the yew maze, planted in 1996. It is truly one of my "follies" and stands as a monument to Timmy's patience and understanding. It was built to house Blot Kerr Wilson's amazing displays of my shell collection, which had been piling up for years. Our initials and those of the children, together with the date the house was built, are included in the pattern of the shells. We bought the Gothic-style windows (above) from an architectural salvage yard.*

chance I was leafing through *Gardens Illustrated* magazine and found an article about a wild and wonderful girl named Blot Kerr Wilson, who adored shells and had decorated every available surface in her semi-detached home with shells—including the loo, bathroom, corridor. I telephoned her instantly—no reply, just an answering machine, and I left a breathless message: "Call me back. If a man answers, put the phone down." Blot came, we schemed, and she started work on the great project.

Very soon I knew that she was going to create a masterpiece, much, much more artistic than I would ever have made it had I had the time. It took five months to complete. Blot's friends, Ben and Purdy, came to help. and in the end it was completed on October 26, 1995, one day before our 25th wedding anniversary. The shell house now stands as a monument to Timmy's patience in putting up with me all these years!

In winter, we get super, freshly dug parsnips that Haulie brings in old sacks, still covered with clay. I explain to the students the importance of buying root vegetables with the clay on; they keep better, and taste better. Then there are the turnips, early Brussels sprouts, winter carrots and leeks, Chinese and Jerusalem artichokes, plenty to comfort and nourish. The rutabagas are particularly sweet, sprinkled with caramelized onions and freshly chopped parsley—even the most ardent vegetable snobs will melt!

Mr. Fitzsimmons brings us his gorgeous free-range chickens, and Nora Aherne rears us tasty ducks, geese, and turkeys, all raised naturally, of course. You can imagine how many we get through with forty-plus students, and we have a huge turkey for our Christmas feast. Christmas is always a big family gathering— maybe thirty or more of us congregate with Myrtle and Ivan at Ballymaloe House. The Christmas meal is a grand affair: oysters and champagne around the fire; roast turkey with buttery herb stuffing, Brussels sprouts, cranberry sauce, and our favorite bread sauce; then moist plum pudding and brandy butter. We pile up the presents under the tree, and, after lunch is finished, the youngest child picks a present and gives it to Granda, the eldest. Then everybody gets one and so the process goes on and on—until we're all ready for tea. We play country house games the children love, like Sardines and Post Office. Eileen decorates our conservatory at Kinoith with lots of holly and pine cones, and we hand-string great rafts of chiles, nuts, and citrus fruit. Lemons, kumquats, and oranges ripen in the conservatory. The Meyer lemons are exquisite and, occasionally, I'll pick one for a very special friend. It's a serious bit of one upmanship to have a home-grown lemon for a gin and tonic!

Just before Christmas, students from our second three-month course prepare to leave. At first they had to job-hunt for themselves. Now that the School is better recognized, through the grand work of our talented ex-students, we are approached by people from all over the world. I'm a member of the International Association of Culinary Professionals (the IACP) and they have a vast directory of contacts. If someone needs a chef in Sri Lanka or in Dublin, they'll contact us. If a student in South Africa hears of an opportunity, they will fax back to the School. One boy was made Chalet Boy of the Year a couple of years ago, and we were thrilled when our daughter Lydia was chosen as Chalet Girl of the Year by Simply Ski. At the outset we had to ask potential employers to consider our students, who'd have to pay their own fares to attend an interview; now companies fly out to visit us. Very gratifying.

Winter in the garden is a period of quiet, when we scan the seed catalogues and decide what we'd like to plant for the coming season. Not much happens around the farm. We tidy up, and clean out the potting shed. If it's mild, we propagate, plants are divided in the herbaceous border, and pruning has to be done. If we get snow, it's a huge excitement for a couple of days; if we get snow for a week the whole place nearly comes to a standstill. I now have a wood-burning stove in the School, and one for our own winter hearth, too.

(TOP) *At Ballymaloe we have a little sprinkle of snow most winters.*

(ABOVE) *Purple Brussels sprouts look great, but the variety I grew did not taste as good as our green ones.*

(ABOVE) *In the lean winter months the rose bower provides a strong architectural feature in the garden when there is little in bloom.*

(LEFT) *It is a joy to watch the ducks on the pond at the end of Lydia's garden.*

(BELOW) *We decorate the Bay tree with chillies to cheer us up in the winter.*

In the flower garden, the winter sweet and the mahonia in the part we call the pleasure garden, near the potting shed, smell intoxicatingly delicious, as does the *Daphne odorata* by the garden gate. Under the office and the larder windows in front of the School there are winter-flowering rhododendrons, which burst into flower each year, rewarding me when little else is in bloom. The crop from our vegetable garden is reduced to sprouting broccoli and kale, still producing abundantly throughout January, and then we have lots of corn salad and mysticana to liven up our winter salads.

As the New Year is ushered in, I start to think about our plans for the coming months. There's time to try out new ideas at home in my own kitchen, and to develop themes for new courses to run at the School. I will always want to expand the range of courses we offer. Of course, there are some of the old favorites, but it is important to be able to put in new ones and whatever takes my fancy that particular year.

Carrot and Cumin Soup

SERVES ABOUT 6

I tablespoon cumin seeds
3 tablespoons butter
I¹/₄ pounds carrots, chopped
(about 5 cups)
³/₄ cup chopped onion
I cup chopped potatoes
Salt, freshly ground black pepper, and
sugar
5 cups Homemade Chicken Stock
(see page 184)
5 tablespoons half-and-half (optional)

GARNISH
A little whipped cream or plain yogurt
Freshly toasted and ground cumin seeds
Fresh cilantro leaves

In our area of Ireland, acres and acres of carrots are grown. Piles of them heaped up by the side of the road are a common sight in autumn. This gutsy winter soup tastes great either hot or cold. Don't hesitate to put in a good pinch of sugar—it brings up the flavor.

Heat the cumin seeds in a skillet, just for a minute or two until they smell rich and spicy. Grind in a mortar and pestle or a spice grinder. Melt the butter in a medium-sized saucepan. When it foams, add the chopped vegetables and the cumin seeds. Season with salt, pepper, and sugar. Cover with a buttered paper and a tight-fitting lid. Allow to sweat gently on low heat for about 10 minutes or until the vegetables have softened slightly. Remove the lid. Add the stock, increase the heat, and boil until the vegetables are soft.

Pour into a blender and purée until smooth. Taste and adjust the seasoning. Add a little half-and-half, if necessary.

To serve: garnish each portion with a blob of whipped cream or yogurt, sprinkle with a little ground cumin, and top with a cilantro a leaf.

Spiced Chickpea Soup

SERVES 4–6

I heaping cup dried chickpeas, soaked
overnight in plenty of cold water
6¹/₄ cups Homemade Chicken or
Vegetable Stock (see pages 184-5)
2–3 teaspoons coriander seeds
2–3 teaspoons cumin seeds
4 tablespoons butter
I¹/₄ cups minced onion
5 large cloves garlic, minced
I–2 small hot red chile peppers, seeded
and chopped
¹/₂ teaspoon ground turmeric
6 tablespoons heavy cream
Salt and freshly ground black pepper

GARNISH
Crème fraîche
Fresh cilantro leaves

A winter soup to warm and fill you!

Drain the chickpeas and put them into a saucepan. Cover with the chicken or vegetable stock and bring to a boil. Cover and simmer gently for 45–60 minutes, or until the chickpeas are soft and tender.

Meanwhile, toast the coriander and cumin seeds in a skillet on medium heat for 2–3 minutes, then crush in a mortar and pestle or spice grinder.

Melt the butter in a saucepan. Add the minced onion, the crushed seeds, garlic, and chopped chile. Cook gently for 4–5 minutes. Add the turmeric, stir, and cook for I–2 minutes. Take the pan off the heat. When the chick-peas are soft and tender, mix everything together.

Purée the chickpea mixture with the cream in a blender or food processor. Put back in a saucepan and simmer for 10–20 minutes. If the soup is a little too thick, thin down with extra stock.

Serve in hot soup bowls topped with a little crème fraîche and sprinkled with fresh cilantro leaves.

Winter Vegetable and Bean Soup with Spicy Sausage

SERVES 8–9

$^1/_2$ pound rindless slab bacon, cut into
$^1/_4$-inch lardons
1 tablespoon olive oil
1 $^1/_2$ cups chopped onions
3 cups carrots, cut into $^1/_4$-inch dice
2 cups celery, cut into $^1/_4$-inch dice
1 cup parsnips, cut into $^1/_4$-inch dice
2 cups white part of leeks, cut into
$^1/_4$-inch slices
1 kabanos sausage, cut into $^1/_8$-inch slices
A 14-ounce can tomatoes, chopped
1$^1/_3$ cups dried white beans, cooked
Salt, freshly ground black pepper, and sugar
7$^1/_2$ cups Homemade Chicken Stock
(see page 184)

GARNISH
2 tablespoons chopped fresh parsley,

This comforting soup makes good use of all the winter produce from the vegetable garden, and we make huge pots of it. I usually keep some in the freezer. Kabanos is a thin, garlicky, Polish sausage; it gives the soup a gutsy, slightly smoky flavor.

Blanch the bacon lardons, refresh, and dry well. Put the olive oil in a saucepan, add the bacon, and sauté over medium heat until it becomes crisp and golden. Add the chopped onions, carrots, and celery. Cover and sweat for 5 minutes. Next, add the diced parsnip and finely sliced leeks. Cover and sweat for 5 more minutes. Add the sliced sausage, chopped tomatoes and beans to the pan. Season with salt, pepper, and sugar. Add the chicken stock and continue to cook until all the vegetables are tender, about 20 minutes. Taste and correct the seasoning.

To serve, sprinkle with the chopped parsley and serve with lots of crusty brown bread.

Thai Chicken, Galangal, and Cilantro Soup

SERVES 8

4 cups Homemade Chicken Stock
(see page 184)
4 kaffir lime leaves
2-inch piece of galangal, or 1-inch piece
of fresh ginger, peeled and sliced
4 tablespoons fish sauce (*nam pla*)
6 tablespoons freshly squeezed
lemon juice
$^1/_2$ pound skinless boneless chicken
breast, finely sliced
1 cup canned coconut milk (the
Chaokoh brand is the best)
2–3 hot red Thai chile peppers
About $^1/_3$ cup fresh cilantro leaves

A particularly delicious example of how fast and easy a Thai soup can be.

Put the chicken stock, lime leaves, galangal (or ginger), fish sauce, and lemon juice into a saucepan. Bring to a boil, stirring all the time. Add the chicken and coconut milk. Continue to cook over high heat until the chicken is just cooked, about 1–2 minutes.

Crush the chiles with a knife or Chinese chopper and add to the soup with the cilantro leaves just a few seconds before ladling it into hot bowls. Serve immediately.

A Plate of Smoked Fish with Horseradish Mayonnaise and Sweet Dill Mayonnaise

SERVES 4

A selection of smoked fish fillets—
salmon, mackerel, trout, eel, tuna, and
whitefish

ACCOMPANIMENT
Horseradish Mayonnaise (see page 186)
Sweet Dill Mayonnaise (see page 187)

GARNISH
Segments of lemon
Sprigs of watercress or arugula leaves

Occasionally we serve just three different types of smoked fish—for example, salmon, mussels, and trout—on tiny rounds of brown yeast bread, topped with a little frill of Red Leaf lettuce. A little blob of Pickled Cucumbers goes with Bill Casey's smoked salmon; homemade Sweet Dill Mayonnaise is delicious with Frank Hederman's marinated smoked mussels; and Horseradish Mayonnaise with a sprig of watercress complement the pink smoked trout or herring from Sally Barnes. All these delicious morsels make a perfect light appetizer.

Thinly slice the salmon down; allow one slice per person. Cut the mackerel into diamond-shaped pieces. Divide the trout into large flakes. Skin and slice the eel. Slice the tuna and the whitefish thinly.

To serve, choose four large plates and drizzle each one with Sweet Dill Mayonnaise. Divide the smoked fish among the plates and arrange appetizingly. Put a blob of Horseradish Mayonnaise on each plate. Garnish with a lemon wedge and sprigs of watercress or arugula leaves.

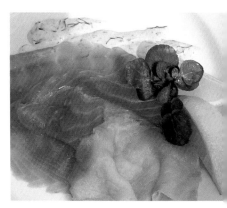

Soused Herring, Pickled Cucumbers, and Sweet Dill Mayonnaise

SERVES 16 (OR 8 AS A MAIN COURSE)

8 fresh herrings
I onion, thinly sliced
I teaspoon whole black peppercorns
6 whole cloves
I teaspoon salt
I teaspoon sugar
I¹/₄ cups white wine vinegar
I bay leaf

Pickled Cucumbers (see page 187)
Sweet Dill Mayonnaise (see page 187)

We get masses of herring brought into Ballycotton, although the season for them is short. This one of the many ways in which we use them.

Preheat the oven to 270°F.

Clean, wash, and fillet the herrings, making sure there are no bones—a tall order with herring, but do your best. Roll up the fillets, skin-side out, and pack tightly into a heavy casserole. Sprinkle over the onion, peppercorns, cloves, salt, sugar, vinegar, and bay leaf. Bring to a boil on top of the stove, then put into the preheated oven to cook for 30–45 minutes. Allow to get quite cold. Soused herring will keep for 7–10 days in the refrigerator.

To serve: put one or two fillets of soused herring on a plate and surround with three little mounds of Pickled Cucumbers, zigzagged with Sweet Dill Mayonnaise. Fresh crusty bread is a must!

151

Seared Beef Salad with Crispy Onions and Horseradish Mayonnaise

SERVES 6

Selection of salad greens

DRESSING
4 tablespoons extra virgin olive oil
1 tablespoon white wine vinegar
$1/4$ teaspoon Lakeshore or other good grainy mustard
1 teaspoon chopped fresh herbs (thyme, parsley, and tarragon would be good)
Salt and freshly ground pepper

CRISPY ONIONS
1 large onion
Milk
Good quality oil or beef drippings for deep frying
All-purpose flour seasoned with salt and pepper

6 or 18 slices of beef tenderloin, cut $1/4$ inch thick—use 1 slice per person from the mid tenderloin or 3 slices each from the tapered end
Salt and freshly ground black pepper
Olive oil

GARNISH
Horseradish Mayonnaise (see page 186)
A few fresh arugula leaves
Freshly cracked black pepper

This is a quick and easy salad that can also be served as a main course. Freshly grated horseradish gives the sauce a good kick, and if you want it to be pungent just add more! If you cannot buy horseradish in your local market, it is well worth growing your own, but watch it carefully, as it spreads like mad. Strips of roasted red sweet pepper and crumbled blue cheese are also a good alternative topping.

Wash and dry the salad greens. Make the dressing by whisking all the ingredients together in a bowl. Season well.

To prepare the crispy onions, slice the onion horizontally into $1/4$-inch rings. Separate the rings and keep covered with the milk until needed. Just before serving, heat oil to 350°F. Toss the rings, a few at a time, in well-seasoned flour. Deep-fry until golden, drain on paper towels and keep hot.

Heat a ridged cast-iron grill pan on high heat. Season the beef on both sides with salt, pepper, and a drizzle of olive oil. Sear the beef on the hot grill pan, first in one direction and then the other, to give a criss-cross effect. Toss the salad greens in just enough dressing to make the leaves glisten.

Just before serving, divide the salad among the warm plates, piling the leaves up in the center. Arrange the seared beef around the leaves. Dribble a little Horseradish Mayonnaise over each slice of beef. Put a clump of hot crispy onions on top of the salad. Serve immediately, with an arugula leaf or two on each plate and a little sprinkling of freshly cracked pepper.

Cloyne Black Pudding with Glazed Apples and Grainy Mustard Sauce

SERVES 4

GLAZED APPLES
2 apples
I tablespoon sugar
2 tablespoons butter
Juice of $1/4$–$1/2$ lemon

Grainy Mustard Sauce (see page 182)

Butter
3 or 4 slices of black pudding, $1/2$ inch thick, per person (we use Kirrane's from Cloyne, or Clonakilty Black Pudding)

GARNISH
Fresh flat-leaf parsley

Black pudding, which is what we call blood sausage, is traditional Irish breakfast food. My brother Rory created this combination. In Ireland, we have a national competition for the best black pudding and, as a happy consequence, regional differences are preserved and producers vie to keep up their very high standards. We get our pudding from Kirrane's in Cloyne, which is just 2 miles from us, or use Clonakilty Black Pudding, which can be bought in the U.S. If you cannot find it, use the French boudin noir.

Peel and core the apples and cut neatly into $1/4$-inch slices. Melt the butter in a sauté pan and, when it foams, add the apple slices. Turn to coat gently in the butter. Add the sugar and lemon juice. Cook slowly for about 5 minutes or until the apples are glazed in a shiny syrup. Keep warm.

Next make the Mustard Sauce.

Melt a little butter in a skillet and cook the slices of black pudding on both sides on medium heat until heated through. Don't let the slices get too crusty on the outside.

To serve: divide the warm apple slices among four hot plates. Arrange the black pudding on the apples and spoon a little Mustard Sauce carefully over the top. Garnish each with a sprig of flat-leaf parsley and serve immediately.

Fresh Cheese Ravioli with Parsley Pesto and Tomato Fondue

SERVES 8

PASTA—MAKES 1 POUND 5 OUNCES
3 cups all-purpose flour
1 teaspoon salt (optional)
3–4 eggs, preferably free-range

1 cup Homemade Cheese
(see page 94) or soft goat cheese
3/4 cup freshly grated Parmesan
cheese (Parmigiano Reggiano)
2 tablespoons minced parsley
Salt and freshly ground black pepper
Grated nutmeg

Tomato Fondue (see page 182)
1 cup heavy cream
3 tablespoons butter
3/4 cup freshly grated Parmesan cheese
Parsley Pesto (see page 186)

GARNISH
Fresh flat-leaf parsley

Pasta machines, either hand-cranked or with an electric motor, are well worth buying if you make pasta on a regular basis. We serve these ravioli with all sorts of garnishes—roasted red sweet pepper, chargrilled eggplant, buttered cabbage, black olives... The possibilities are unlimited.

First make the pasta. Sift the flour into a bowl and add the salt if using. Whisk the eggs together, Make a well in the center of the flour and add most of the egg. Mix into a dough with your hand, adding the remaining egg if you need it. The pasta should just come together, but should not stick to your hand—if it does, add a little more flour. (If it is very much too wet, it is very difficult to get it right.) Knead for a few minutes until smooth, then let rest on a plate, covered with an upturned bowl, for 1 hour to relax.

Divide the dough in half and roll out one piece at a time into a very thin sheet, keeping the other piece covered. You ought to be able to read newsprint through the pasta. A long thin rolling pin is a great advantage, but you can manage perfectly well with an ordinary domestic rolling pin. Don't let the pasta dry out; cover it with a dish towel while you make the filling.

Mix the cheese with the freshly grated Parmesan and minced parsley. Season well with salt, pepper, and a little nutmeg.

To assemble, put a sheet of pasta on the work top and brush lightly with cold water. Put teaspoons of filling about 1½ inches apart on the pasta. Lay another identical-sized sheet of pasta on top, seal the edges loosely, and press out the air gently with the side of your hand. Cut into squares with a pastry wheel or stamp out rounds with a fluted cutter.

The ravioli can be cooked immediately or refrigerated for a few hours. However, this delicate filling is perishable, so the ravioli should be cooked on the same day. Bring 4½ quarts water to a fast rolling boil and add 2 tablespoons salt. Shoot in the ravioli and put the lid back on the saucepan until the water returns to a boil.

Meanwhile, heat the Tomato Fondue. Put the cream and butter into a wide sauté pan and allow to bubble for a minute. The ravioli will be cooked in about 5 minutes. Test, then drain and add to the bubbling cream. Add the Parmesan cheese. Toss gently until the ravioli is nicely coated.

Serve with Tomato Fondue and a little Parsley Pesto and garnished with flat-leaf parsley.

Gratin of Cod with Imokilly Cheddar and Mustard

SERVES 6

6 pieces of cod fillet, 6 ounces each
Salt and freshly ground black pepper
2 cups grated aged Irish Cheddar cheese
I tablespoon Dijon mustard
4 tablespoons heavy cream

Piquant Beets (see page 168)

This is one of the simplest and most delicious fish dishes we know. If cod is unavailable, haddock, hake, or striped mullet are also great. We use Imokilly Cheddar cheese from our local creamery at Mogeely, but you can use any good, well-flavored aged Cheddar.

Preheat the oven to 350°F.

Season the fish with salt and pepper. Arrange the pieces in a single layer in a buttered baking dish measuring about 8 by 10 inches (it should be posh enough to bring to the table). Grate the cheese, mix with the mustard and cream, and spread carefully over the fish. (It can be prepared ahead and refrigerated at this point.) Bake in the preheated oven for about 20 minutes or until the fish is cooked and the top is golden and bubbly. Flash under the broiler, if necessary.

Serve with hot Piquant Beets.

Salmon with Swiss Chard

SERVES 6

A ¹/₂-pound piece of salmon fillet (get the thick center of a large salmon and ask the fishmonger to remove the skin)
Salt and freshly ground black pepper
³/₄ pound Swiss chard or ruby chard
4 tablespoons olive oil
I large onion, thinly sliced
A (I¹/₂-inch cube of fresh ginger, peeled and first cut into very thin slices and then into very fine slivers, or shredded on a grater
8 canned plum tomatoes, chopped
I teaspoon sugar
¹/₂ cup thick canned coconut milk (we use the Chaokoh brand)

Madhur Jaffrey introduced me to this combination, which she discovered in the Philippines. It is a great recipe for a dinner party.

Remove any bones from the fish with tweezers. Cut the salmon fillet into six portions. Season the fish with salt and pepper and set aside while you prepare the chard. Swiss chard has a central stem bordered by spinach-like leaves. Strip the leaf from the stem. Cut the leafy section, crosswise, into ¹/₄ inch wide strips. Set aside. Then slice the stems crosswise into ¹/₈-inch wide strips.

Heat the oil in a very wide sauté pan or large skillet on medium heat. Add the onion, ginger, and chard stems. Sauté, stirring occasionally, for about 5 minutes. Add the chopped tomatoes and the sugar and continue to sauté for 4–5 minutes. Add the coconut milk and I¹/₂ cups of water and season well with salt and some pepper. Stir, bring to a boil and then simmer on low heat for a minute. (The recipe can be prepared ahead up to this point.)

Just before serving, bring the sauce to simmering point again. Stir in the chard leaves and arrange the salmon pieces in a single layer over the top of the sauce. Spoon some of the sauce over the fish. Cover with a tight-fitting lid and simmer for 4–5 minutes, or until the salmon is just cooked through.

To serve, lift the fish and chard onto a hot serving dish. Spoon the sauce over the top of the fish and serve immediately.

Steak and Oyster Pie

SERVES 4–6

1¹/₂ pounds boneless beef, such as round steak, best chuck, or thick rib steak
Salt and freshly ground black pepper
2 tablespoons butter
1¹/₂ cups chopped onion
1 tablespoon all-purpose flour
2¹/₂ cups Homemade Beef Stock (see page 185)

3 cups sliced mushrooms
12 Native Irish or Pacific oysters
Roux, if necessary (see page 182)

¹/₄ recipe quantity Puff Pastry (see page 182)
Egg wash

This may seem to be a modern combination, but, in fact, it is an old classic that dates back to a time when oysters were ten a penny and were put in to bulk out the steak!

Cut the beef into 1¹/₂-inch cubes and season with salt and pepper. Melt a little butter in a skillet and sear the meat over high heat. Remove the meat to a plate. Add the onions to the skillet and cook for 5–6 minutes. Take the pan from the heat and stir in the flour. Return to the heat and cook for 1 minute. Blend in the stock. Return the meat and bring to a boil. Transfer to a flameproof casserole, cover, and simmer on low heat for 1¹/₂–2 hours. Alternatively, cook in a preheated 325°F oven for 1¹/₂–2 hours.

Meanwhile, sauté the mushrooms in the remaining butter on high heat. Season with salt and pepper and set aside. Shuck the oysters and put in a bowl with their juice. When the meat is tender, thicken the cooking juices slightly with roux, if necessary. Add the mushrooms and oysters with their juice and taste for seasoning. Boil for 3 or 4 minutes. Allow to get cold, then put into a 5-cup capacity deep-dish pie pan or casserole.

Preheat the oven to 475°F. Roll out the pastry to about ¹/₄ inch thickness and cover the pie. Flute the edges and decorate with pastry leaves. Brush with egg wash. Bake in the preheated oven for 10 minutes, then reduce the temperature to 375°F and bake for a further 15–20 minutes or until the pastry is puffed and golden. Serve hot.

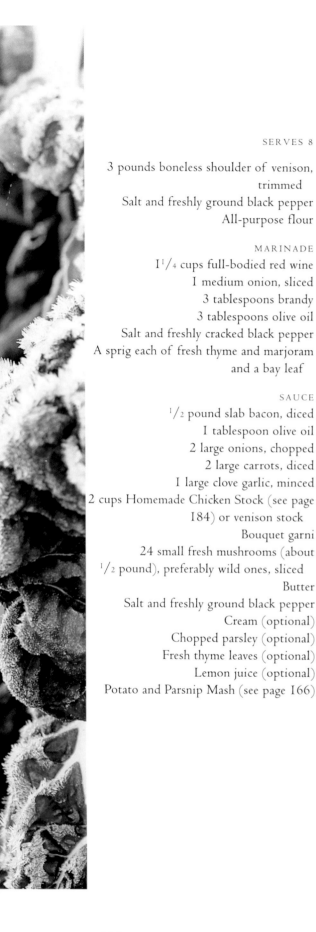

Venison Stew with Potato and Parsnip Mash

SERVES 8

3 pounds boneless shoulder of venison, trimmed
Salt and freshly ground black pepper
All-purpose flour

MARINADE
1¹/₄ cups full-bodied red wine
I medium onion, sliced
3 tablespoons brandy
3 tablespoons olive oil
Salt and freshly cracked black pepper
A sprig each of fresh thyme and marjoram and a bay leaf

SAUCE
¹/₂ pound slab bacon, diced
I tablespoon olive oil
2 large onions, chopped
2 large carrots, diced
I large clove garlic, minced
2 cups Homemade Chicken Stock (see page 184) or venison stock
Bouquet garni
24 small fresh mushrooms (about ¹/₂ pound), preferably wild ones, sliced
Butter
Salt and freshly ground black pepper
Cream (optional)
Chopped parsley (optional)
Fresh thyme leaves (optional)
Lemon juice (optional)
Potato and Parsnip Mash (see page 166)

Our venison comes from the Ballinatray estate near Youghal. The sweet flavor of parsnips works well with venison.

Dice the venison and season well. Put in a bowl and add the mixed marinade ingredients. Cover and refrigerate for 12–24 hours. Drain the meat well, pat it dry on paper towels, and turn lightly in flour seasoned with salt and pepper.

Preheat the oven to 300°F.

Brown the cubes of bacon for the sauce in the olive oil in a skillet. Cook slowly at first to render out the fat, then raise the heat to get them crisp on the outside. Transfer to a flameproof casserole using a slotted spoon.

Brown the venison in the sizzling fat and add to the casserole. Brown the onions, carrots, and garlic, in batches, transferring each one to the casserole as it is browned. Control the heat carefully or the fat will burn. Pour off any surplus fat, then deglaze the pan with the strained marinade and pour the liquid over the venison. Heat up enough stock just to cover the meat and vegetables in the casserole and pour it over them. Add the bouquet garni. Bring to a gentle simmer on top of the stove, then cover tightly and transfer to the preheated oven. Continue to cook until the venison is tender and melting. Test after 1¹/₂ hours, but it may take up to 2¹/₂ hours.

For best results, we cook this casserole a day ahead and then reheat it the next. This improves the flavor and ensures that the venison is tender.

Sauté the sliced mushrooms in a little butter. Season with salt and pepper and add to the stew. I sometimes add a little cream and some chopped parsley and thyme leaves, too. Finally, taste the sauce; it may need seasoning and perhaps a squeeze of lemon juice. It often benefits from a pinch of sugar or a spoonful of red-currant jelly (be careful not to use too much).

Serve with Potato and Parsnip Mash.

Pheasant with Jerusalem Artichokes

Pheasants adore Jerusalem artichokes; most of the large estates in Ireland plant a special patch as a treat for them. It seemed logical to cook them together, and indeed it has turned out to be a very good marriage of flavors. Chicken or guinea fowl can also be cooked in this manner.

SERVES 4

2 tablespoons butter
I plump pheasant
2 pounds Jerusalem artichokes
Salt and freshly ground black pepper

GARNISH
Curly or flat-leaf parsley, chopped

Preheat the oven to 350°F.

Smear a little butter on the breast of the pheasant and brown it in a flameproof casserole over low heat. Meanwhile, peel the artichokes and slice into ¹/₂-inch pieces. Remove the pheasant from the casserole. Add a little butter to the pot and toss the slices of Jerusalem artichoke in it. Season with salt and pepper and sprinkle a tablespoon of water over the top. Then replace the pheasant, tucking it right down into the sliced artichokes so they come up around the sides of the bird. Cover with a buttered piece of parchment paper and the lid of the casserole. Cook for I–I¹/₄ hours.

Remove the pheasant as soon as it is cooked. Strain off the cooking juices and skim them of fat if necessary (usually there is no fat). The juices of the pheasant will have flavored the artichokes deliciously. Arrange the artichokes on a hot serving dish. Carve the pheasant into four portions and arrange on top. The artichokes always break up a little—that is their nature. Spoon the juices over the pheasant and artichokes.

Serve sprinkled with chopped parsley.

Roast Stuffed Duck with Beets

SERVES 4

I free-range duck, weighing about
4 pounds
Homemade Duck Stock (see page 185)

SAGE AND ONION STUFFING
¹/₂ cup minced onion
3 tablespoons butter
2 cups soft white bread crumbs
I tablespoon chopped fresh sage
Salt and freshly ground black pepper

Applesauce (see page 187)

Piquant Beets (see page 169)

Nora Ahearne rears us the most beautiful free-range ducks and geese. Make enquiries in your area and, if you find a treasure like Nora, someone willing to rear poultry of this quality for you, be prepared to pay a premium price for a bird—it will be worth every penny. Beets go particularly well with roast goose and duck, and also with roast pork.

To make the stuffing, sweat the onions in the butter on low heat for 5–10 minutes until soft but not colored. Add the bread crumbs and sage. Season with salt and pepper. Unless you plan to cook the duck immediately, let the stuffing get cold.

Preheat the oven to 350°F.

When the stuffing is quite cold, season the cavity of the duck and spoon in the stuffing. Roast in the preheated oven for about I¹/₂ hours.

Meanwhile, make the Applesauce.

When the duck is cooked, remove to a serving dish and let rest while you make the gravy. Heat the stock. Degrease the cooking juices (keeping the duck fat for roasted or sauté potatoes). Add the stock to the juices in the roasting pan and bring to a boil, then taste and season if necessary. Strain the gravy into a sauce boat.

Serve the duck with warm applesauce, beets, and gravy.

Sweet-Sour Pork with Prunes, Raisins, Pine Nuts, and Polenta

SERVES 8–10

4 pounds boneless shoulder or leg of
pork (fresh ham), cubed
5 tablespoons olive oil
Sea salt
$^3/_4$ cup red wine vinegar
Freshly ground black pepper
36 prunes, plumped in water and drained
$^1/_3$ cup raisins, plumped in hot water
and drained
$^1/_3$ cup pine nuts, toasted
2 tablespoons sugar
$1^1/_2$ ounces bittersweet chocolate, grated

MARINADE
6 juniper berries
10 black peppercorns
2 bay leaves
$^1/_2$ teaspoon fresh thyme leaves
I carrot, chopped
I onion, chopped
I stalk celery, chopped
3 cups or more dry red wine
$^1/_4$ cup red wine vinegar

ACCOMPANIMENT
Polenta (see page 183)

Jo Bettoja, whose food I adore, served us this rich sweet-sour stew in her home in Rome. It is an old family recipe for wild boar that has been passed down through the generations. Timmy and I loved the rich gutsy flavor, so she kindly shared her recipe with us.

Mix all the ingredients for the marinade together in a bowl. Add the cubes of pork and stir well. Cover and let marinate for 48 hours in the refrigerator. Stir every now and then during this period.

Preheat the oven to 325°F.

Drain the meat, and reserve the marinade and the vegetables. Dry the meat on paper towels. Heat 4 tablespoons of the olive oil in a skillet on high heat. Brown the meat on all sides, then transfer the pieces to a casserole and season with salt. Add a little more oil to the skillet and cook the marinated vegetables for 10–15 minutes or until the onion is soft. Add a few tablespoons of the marinade to prevent the vegetables from burning. Add to the casserole. Deglaze the skillet with the reserved marinade plus $^1/_4$ cup of the vinegar. Bring to a boil and scrape into the casserole. Add $^1/_2$ teaspoon freshly ground black pepper. Cover the casserole and cook in the preheated oven until the meat is tender, about $1^1/_2$ hours.

Remove the meat to a bowl and strain the sauce into a saucepan. Press the vegetables through the strainer to get the last of the juices. Add the prunes, raisins, and pine nuts to the sauce.

In another small saucepan, simmer the remaining red wine vinegar with the sugar for 4 minutes, then add to the sauce with the chocolate and the meat. Bring to a boil slowly and simmer for 15 minutes. Taste and adjust the seasoning if necessary.

Serve with soft Polenta and follow with a green salad.

Black-Eyed Peas and Chickpea Stew

This recipe is suitable for vegetarians and vegans. We make lots of this kind of combination stew. Of course,. you can use canned beans if you are in a hurry, but they are more expensive.

SERVES 6

1 1/2 cups dried black-eyed peas
1 cup dried chickpeas
6 tablespoons sunflower or peanut oil
1 teaspoon cumin seeds
1-inch piece of cinnamon stick
3/4 cup chopped onions
4 cloves garlic, minced
3 cups thinly sliced mushrooms
2 1/2 cups tomatoes, peeled and chopped,
or a 16-ounce can crushed tomatoes
2 teaspoons ground coriander
1 teaspoon ground cumin
1/2 teaspoon ground turmeric
Pinch of sugar
1/4 teaspoon cayenne pepper
1 heaping teaspoon salt (it needs it, so
don't cut down)
Freshly ground black pepper
3 tablespoons chopped fresh cilantro
(fresh parsley can be substituted,
though the flavor is not at all the
same)
1 heaping tablespoon fresh mint leaves

Soak the beans and chickpeas separately in plenty of cold water overnight. The next day, drain, cover again with fresh water, and simmer for 30–45 minutes or until just cooked.

Heat the oil in a sauté pan over medium-high heat. When hot, put in the whole cumin seeds and the cinnamon stick. Let them sizzle for 5–6 seconds. Now put in the onions and garlic. Stir and fry until the onions are just beginning to color at the edge. Put in the mushrooms, and stir and fry until they wilt. Now put in the tomatoes, ground coriander, ground cumin, turmeric, sugar, and cayenne. Stir and cook for a minute. Cover the pan and let this mixture cook on a gentle heat in its own juices for 10 minutes. Remove from the heat.

Drain the beans and the chickpeas, reserving the cooking liquid from each pan. Add to the mushroom base mixture. Add salt, pepper, 2 tablespoons of the cilantro, and 2/3 cup each of the bean and the chickpea cooking liquids. Bring the stew to a boil again. Reduce the heat and simmer for 10–20 minutes or until the beans and chickpeas are tender, stirring occasionally. Remove the cinnamon stick before serving.

Sprinkle with the remaining chopped cilantro and the mint and serve with rice and a green salad.

Tagine of Lamb with Preserved Lemons

SERVES 6

TAGINE

3 pounds boned shoulder of lamb
$^1/_2$ tablespoon ground cinnamon
I teaspoon ground ginger
I teaspoon freshly ground black pepper
Large pinch of saffron threads

4 tablespoons unsalted butter
2 onions, chopped
2 cloves garlic, minced
Salt
I cup raisins, plumped in water and
drained
2 tablespoons honey
3 tablespoons chopped fresh cilantro

I Moroccan Preserved Lemon
(see page 166)
$^1/_2$ cup sliced almonds
I tablespoon oil

The word "tagine" refers to the distinctive earthenware cooking pot of Morocco, and to the stew-like dishes cooked in it. These can be based on meat, fish, or vegetables. I lugged my precious tagine, and its brazier, all the way from Marrakesh. Without question it is the most expensive tagine in the whole of Ireland, because although I got a bargain in the Medina, I had to pay excess baggage at the airport and the Moroccans would not settle for my leftover dirham—they wanted pounds sterling or dollars and would not part with the tagine until they got them!

Trim the lamb, discarding the excess fat. Cut into I$^1/_2$-inch cubes. Mix the cinnamon, ginger, pepper, and saffron with 4 tablespoons water. Toss the lamb in this mixture. If you have time, let it marinate for up to 24 hours.

Melt the butter in a wide pan. Add the lamb, onions, garlic, salt, and just enough water to cover. Bring to a boil, then cover and reduce the heat to give a gentle simmer. Cook for about I hour, turning the lamb occasionally, until the meat is meltingly tender. Then add the raisins, honey, and half the cilantro. Continue simmering, with the pan uncovered, for a further 30 minutes or so, until the sauce is thick and unctuous. Taste and adjust the seasoning.

While the tagine is cooking, scoop the flesh out of the Preserved Lemon and discard. Chop up the peel. Fry the almonds and the lemon peel in the oil until golden brown. Drain on paper towels. Sprinkle the lemon peel,

Roast Woodcock with Sweet Geranium Jelly

SERVES 4

4 woodcock
4 tablespoons melted butter
Salt and freshly ground black pepper
Pork caul fat or sliced bacon

4 slices of bread, large enough for the
birds to sit on
Butter

I tablespoon brandy (optional)

GARNISH
Sprigs of watercress or a small bouquet
of fresh herbs

Sweet Geranium Jelly (see page 188)

Woodcock and snipe are highly regarded, not only for their delicious flesh, but also for their innards—with the exception of the gizzard, which is removed before the birds are roasted. Be sure thye are plucked carefully, head and all, because woodcock or snipe are traditionally served trussed with their own long beak. They are best if hung for 4–5 days.

Preheat the oven to 450°F.

Remove the gizzard from each bird by making a small incision in the thin skin of the abdomen, slightly to the right of the center, near the vent. Locate the gizzard with a skewer or trussing needle (this is not as difficult as it sounds—it will feel like a hard lump). Remove and detach from the innards, which should remain in the bird.

Brush the birds with melted butter and season with salt and pepper. Wrap in pork caul or bacon and secure with cotton thread or string.

Toast 4 slices of bread and butter one side. Put the toast, buttered-side down, on a baking pan and put the woodcock on top. Roast in the preheated oven for 18–22 minutes, depending on size. They are usually cooked when the caul fat or bacon is crisp. A tablespoon of brandy can be added to the juices in the roasting pan. Season with salt and pepper and warm through but do not boil.

To serve, arrange the croutons on a hot serving dish, spoon the sauce over, and sit the birds on top. Garnish with sprigs of watercress or a little bouquet of fresh herbs. Serve with Sweet Geranium Jelly.

Rutabaga with Caramelized Onions

SERVES ABOUT 6

2 pounds rutabaga
Salt and lots of freshly ground black
pepper
4–8 tablespoons butter, or
4 tablespoons butter plus
6–8 tablespoons
heavy cream

CARAMELIZED ONIONS
2–3 tablespoons olive oil
I pound onions, thinly sliced

GARNISH
Fresh flat-leaf parsley, finely snipped

Rutabaga is sweetest after it has had a touch of frost. It is unquestionably one of the most underrated of all vegetables.

Peel the rutabaga generously to remove the thick outside skin. Cut into $^3/_4$-inch cubes. Cover with fresh water in a saucepan. Add a good pinch of salt, bring to a boil, and cook until soft.

Meanwhile, make the caramelized onions. Heat the olive oil in a heavy saucepan. Toss in the onions and cook on low heat for whatever length of time it takes for them to soften and caramelize to a golden brown, about 30–45 minutes. Remember to stir occasionally so they brown evenly. If you cannot be bothered to cook them long and slowly like this, put I–I$^1/_2$ tablespoons of olive oil, or mixed olive and sunflower oil, into a skillet. Heat to hot but not smoking. Fry a few thinly sliced onion rings at a time, drain in a wire strainer over a stainless steel bowl, and then dry on paper towels. Continue until all the onions are cooked—faster but actually more labor-intensive. Save the onion-flavored oil for sauté potatoes or crostini.

Drain the rutabaga, mash well and beat in the butter and cream if using. Taste and season with lots of freshly ground pepper and more salt if necessary. Sprinkle the caramelized onions over the top. Garnish with the parsley and serve piping hot.

Green Broccoli or Romanesco Cauliflower

SERVES 4

I pound broccoli or Romanesco
cauliflower
1 1/2 teaspoons salt
2 1/2 cups water
Lots of freshly ground black pepper
I–2 tablespoons butter (optional)

The secret of real flavor in broccoli, and the pale green variety of cauliflower called Romanesco, as in many other green vegetables, is not just freshness; they need to be cooked in well-salted water. If you grow your own, cut out the central head, but leave the plant intact; very soon you will have lots of smaller florets. With broccoli don't discard the stems: peel them and cook them. The grated stem is also very good in a broccoli slaw.

Cut off the stem close to the head, then peel and cut into 1/2-inch pieces. If the heads are large, divide into small clusters of florets. Add the salt to the water and bring to a fast boil. Add the stalks first and then the florets. Cook, uncovered, at a rolling boil for 5–6 minutes. Drain while the broccoli still has a bite. Broccoli can be blanched and refreshed earlier in the day and then reheated in a saucepan of boiling salted water just before serving. Taste, season with pepper, and serve immediately. Better still, melt a little butter in a saucepan until it foams, toss the broccoli gently in it, season to taste, and serve immediately.

Curly Kale and its Cousins

SERVES ABOUT 4

I pound curly kale, stems removed
Salt and freshly ground black pepper
Nutmeg, grated (optional)
4 tablespoons butter
1/2 cup heavy cream

Much as I love the winter root vegetables—parsnip, celery root, rutabaga, and so on—I also long for the clean, sharp taste of greens in the late autumn and winter. Kale and the sprouting broccolis satisfy this need deliciously and, in the case of kale, most decoratively. We grow several different varieties apart from curly kale. Some of the leaves are serrated, others crinkly, others almost feathery; they come in the most beautiful shades, from greeny-gray to blue, green, deep purple, cream, and yellow. Red Russian kale is one of our favorites, I can hardly bear to pick the deeply serrated leaves, which look so beautiful in the winter garden covered with frost or in the early morning when the sun shines on the droplets of dew caught on them. The tussle between the cook and gardener in me is at its most acute then.

Put 3 1/2 quarts of water and I tablesoon salt in a large saucepan and bring to a boil. Add the curly kale and boil, uncovered, on high heat until tender: this can vary from 5–10 minutes, depending on the texture. Drain well, then purée in a food processor. Return to the saucepan and season with salt, freshly ground pepper, and a little nutmeg if you fancy. Add a large lump of butter and some cream, bubble, and taste. Serve hot.

Moroccan Preserved Lemons

5 lemons
3 tablespoons pickling salt (pure salt without additives)
Extra freshly squeezed lemon juice from about 3–4 lemons

Preserved lemons are one of those initial "yuk" tastes that later become addictive. Nothing else provides the authentic taste of Morocco in quite the same way. Add to tagines, fish stews, soups, and salad dressing.

Scrub the lemons thoroughly and quarter them from the top to within $^1/_2$ inch of the base. Sprinkle some salt on the flesh, then close and reshape the fruit. Put 2 tablespoons of salt in the bottom of a sterilized canning jar. Pack in the lemons, pressing down gently. Cover them with the extra lemon juice and top up with boiling water. Seal the jar and leave the lemons to mature for 30 days before using. They will keep for up to a year.

Potato and Parsnip Mash

SERVES ABOUT 8

I pound of potatoes suitable for mashing
Salt and freshly ground black pepper
$2^1/_2$ pounds parsnips
$1^1/_4$–$1^1/_2$ half-and-half
About 4 tablespoons butter

GARNISH
2 tablespoons chopped parsley

This is wonderful with Venison Stew (see page 158), as the slightly sweet taste and soft texture balance the meat perfectly.

Scrub the potatoes. Put them into a saucepan of cold water, add a large pinch of salt, and bring to a boil. When the potatoes are about half-cooked (after about 15 minutes), drain off two-thirds of the water. Replace the lid on the saucepan, put on low heat, and let the potatoes steam until they are cooked.

Peel the parsnips and cut into chunks. Cook in boiling, salted water until tender, then drain and mash. Keep warm.

When the potatoes are just cooked, put the milk in a saucepan and bring to a boil. Pull the skins off the potatoes, mash quickly while they are still warm and beat in enough boiling milk to make a fluffy mash. (If you have a large quantity, put the potatoes in the bowl of an electric mixer and beat.) Then add the mashed parsnip with the butter. Taste for seasoning. Serve immediately, or reheat later in a preheated 350°F oven at for about 20–25 minutes.

Serve in a hot dish with a scattering of parsley on top, or, if you like, piled high with Parsnip Chips (see page 127).

Winter Green Salad with Herb Vinaigrette Dressing

Winter salad greens (see right)

WINTER VINAIGRETTE
6 tablespoons extra virgin olive oil
2 tablespoons red wine vinegar
$^1/_2$ teaspoon Irish honey
I teaspoon grainy mustard
Small clove garlic, crushed
2 tablespoons freshley chopped mixed
herbs (parsley, chives, mint,
watercress, thyme)
Salt and freshly ground black pepper

For this salad, use a selection of winter lettuces and salad greens such as butter-head, iceberg, radicchio, curly and Belgian endive, watercress, sorrel, arugula leaves, and winter purslane. The tips of purple sprouting broccoli are also delicious. If you feel like something more robust, include some finely shredded Savoy cabbage and maybe a few shreds of red cabbage, too.

Wash and dry the lettuces and salad greens and tear into bite-sized pieces. Keep the smaller leaves such as purslane, arugula and sorrel whole. Put all the leaves into a deep salad bowl, add the shredded cabbage, and toss it all together.

To make the vinaigrette, put all the ingredients into a jar with a tight-fitting lid , adding salt and pepper to taste. Shake well to emulsify the dressing before use; otherwise, work together all the ingredients in a food processor or blender for a few seconds.

Just before serving, add a little vinaigrette to the salad greens and toss until they are just glistening.

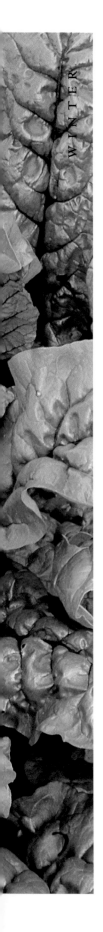

Celery Root and Apple Purée

1¹/₂ pounds celery root, peeled
1 quart milk or water
³/₄ pound apples
1 teaspoon sugar
4 tablespoons heavy cream
1–2 tablespoons butter
Salt and freshly ground black pepper

Celery root, or celeriac, is great with pheasant, venison, duck, or a juicy pork chop. You can also roast them, make them into gratins, soups or even chips.

Cut the peeled celery root into large chunks. Simmer in the milk or lightly salted water until soft and tender, about 15 minutes. Meanwhile, peel and core the apples, cut into quarters, and cook with the sugar and very little water (about 2 teaspoons) in a covered saucepan.

When the celery root is cooked, drain and add to the apple. Purée in a food processor with the cream and a lump of butter until smooth. Taste and season with salt and pepper. This purée can, of course, be prepared ahead. Reheat in a covered dish in a preheated 350°F oven .

Oven-Roasted Winter Root Vegetables

SEE PICTURE RIGHT
About equal volume of parsnips, rutabaga, celery root, and carrot, peeled and cut into ¹/₂-inch cubes
Olive oil
Salt and freshly ground black pepper

GARNISH
Freshly chopped winter herbs—thyme, rosemary, chives, and parsley

In California, many restaurants have wood-burning ovens, which give the food a delicious sweet flavor. We now have one, too, in the garden café.

Preheat the oven to 400°F.

Drizzle olive oil generously over the cubed vegetables and season well with salt and pepper. Spread them in a single layer in one or more roasting pans. Roast, uncovered, stirring occasionally, until cooked and just beginning to caramelize. Take care: a little color makes the vegetables taste sweeter, but too dark they become bitter. Serve sprinkled with the herbs.

Chinese Artichokes

SERVES 6

1 pound Chinese artichokes
2–4 tablespoons butter
Salt and freshly ground black pepper
Chopped parsley, or a mixture of parsley and fresh marjoram

Chinese artichokes, also called Japanese artichokes, knotroot, and chorogi, look beautiful, but need careful washing. The flavor, though, makes it worth the effort. Growing the vegetable is rewarding as it increases every year.

Wash the artichokes, preferably as soon as they have been dug up. Trim them. Melt a little butter in a saucepan and add the artichokes. Season with salt and freshly ground pepper, add a few tablespoons of water, and cover with a buttered piece of parchment paper and the lid of the saucepan. Cook on medium heat for 5–15 minutes or until they are just tender. Add a little chopped parsley, or a mixture of parsley and marjoram, and serve.

Piquant Beets

SERVES 6

1¹/₂ pounds beets, cooked
1 tablespoon butter
A few drops of freshly squeezed
lemon juice
²/₃–³/₄ cup heavy cream
Salt and freshly ground black pepper
Sugar

Peel the cooked beets (wearing rubber gloves if you are vain). Chop the beets into cubes.

Melt the butter in a sauté pan, add the beet, and toss. Add the freshly squeezed lemon juice and cream and bubble for a few minutes. Season with salt, pepper, and sugar. Taste, and add a little more lemon juice if necessary. Serve immediately.

Christmas Semifreddo with Raisins and Marrons Glacés

SERVES 10–12

6 tablespoons Jamaican rum
$^1/_2$ cup raisins
4 free-range eggs
$^1/_4$ cup sugar
I pound canned chestnut purée
I teaspoon pure vanilla extract
$^1/_2$ pound marrons glacés, roughly
chopped
I$^3/_4$ cups heavy cream

Chocolate Caraque (see page 189)

DECORATION
Whipped cream
6–8 marrons glacés

Sprig of holly
Confectioners' sugar

YOU WILL NEED
A 5-pint dome-shaped mold

This is a wonderfully festive Italian semifreddo.

Line the mold with a double thickness of plastic wrap.

Put the rum and raisins in a small saucepan and warm until the rum almost reaches boiling point, then remove from the heat. Let the raisins plump up and cool in the rum.

Meanwhile, separate the eggs and beat the yolks with the sugar until light and fluffy. Stir the chestnut purée, vanilla, cold plump raisins with the rum, and roughly chopped marrons glacés into the egg yolks. Mix gently but thoroughly, then refrigerate while you prepare the cream and egg whites.

Whip the cream and chill. Beat the egg whites stiffly. Fold the whipped cream into the rum and raisin mixture, then fold in the stiffly beaten egg whites. Pour gently into the lined mold. Cover and freeze for at least 8 hours or overnight.

To serve: unmold onto a chilled serving dish. Remove the plastic wrap. Decorate with whipped cream, marrons glacés, and chocolate caraque. Top with a sprig of holly, then dredge with confectioners' sugar.

Chocolate Cases filled with Silky Chocolate Mousse

SERVES 10

CHOCOLATE CASES
8 ounces bittersweet chocolate (with a high percentage of cocoa butter)

CHOCOLATE MOUSSE
8 ounces bittersweet chocolate (with a high percentage of cocoa butter)
I tablespoon unsalted butter
$^2/_3$ cup water
I tablespoon Jamaican rum
6 medium or 4 extra large free-range eggs, separated

DECORATION
Whipped cream
Chocolate Caraque (see page 189)
Unsweetened cocoa powder

YOU WILL NEED
24 cup-cake cases (use 2 papers for each chocolate case to give extra strength to the sides)

This is really rich, really sinful, and really good!

First make the chocolate cases. Melt the chocolate until smooth in a very low oven or in a bowl set over hot water. Spread the chocolate evenly over the inside of the paper cases with the back of a teaspoon. Check that there are no "see-through" patches when you hold them up to the light (it is a good idea to do a few extra cases to allow for accidents!). Stand each one in a cup in a muffin tin and leave to firm in a cold place. Peel the paper layers off carefully and set aside.

Next make the mousse. Break the chocolate into small pieces and put in a bowl to melt with the butter and water over low heat. Stir gently until melted and completely smooth. Remove from the heat and let cool, then whisk in the rum, if using, and the egg yolks. Beat the egg whites and fold them in. Beat for 5–6 minutes: this makes the mousse smooth and silky. (Even though it sounds like a contradiction, the mousse thickens as it is beaten at the end.) Fill each chocolate case with the mousse. Allow to set in the refrigerator for 5–6 hours or overnight.

Then make the Chocolate Caraque.

To serve: pipe a rosette of softly whipped cream onto each mousse. Top with a few pieces of Caraque. Sift a little unsweetened cocoa powder over the top and serve chilled.

Yogurt and Cardamom Mold with Pomegranate Seeds Perfumed with Rosewater

SERVES 8–10

$^1/_4$ teaspoon green cardamom seeds, freshly ground—you'll need about 8–10 cardamom pods, depending on size
I cup milk
I cup sugar
I cup heavy cream
3 heaping teaspoons unflavored gelatin
2 cups plain yogurt

POMEGRANATE SEEDS WITH ROSEWATER
6–8 pomegranates, depending on size
A little lemon juice
I–2 tablespoons sugar
Rosewater to taste

DECORATION
Sweet geranium or mint leaves

I have got a wonderful Irish rose, called Souvenir de St. Ann's, in Lydia's garden. This rose blooms even in the depths of winter, so I steal a few petals and crystallize them to decorate this and other desserts (see Crystallized Violets, page 48).

In summer you can serve this with sugared strawberries or mango tossed with lime juice. It is also good with Gooseberry and Elderflower Compote (see page 42) or a compote of blood oranges or kumquats (see page 173).

Remove the seeds from the cardamom pods and crush in a mortar and pestle. Put the milk, sugar, and cream into a stainless steel saucepan with the ground cardamom. Stir until the sugar has dissolved and the mixture is warm to the touch. Remove from the heat and let infuse while you dissolve the gelatin.

Put 3 tablespoons of cold water into a small bowl, sprinkle the gelatin over the water, and let soften for a few minutes. Set the bowl in a saucepan of simmering water until the gelatin has dissolved and is completely clear. Add a little of the cardamom-infused milk mixture, stir well, and then mix this into the rest. Whisk the yogurt lightly until smooth and creamy, and stir into the cardamom mixture. Pour into a wide serving dish or a lightly oiled ring mold and chill for several hours to set.

Meanwhile, cut the pomegranates in half around the "equator." Carefully separate the seeds from the membrane. Put the seeds into a bowl, sprinkle with just a little freshly squeezed lemon juice, and add sugar and rosewater to taste. Refrigerate until well chilled.

If the yogurt and cardamom mixture has been set in a ring mold, unmold onto a chilled plate. Fill the center with chilled, rose-scented pomegranate seeds. Decorate with sweet geranium or mint leaves, or, even prettier, with crystallized rose petals.

Pure Vanilla Ice Cream with Kumquat Compote and Chocolate Diamonds

SERVES 6–8

VANILLA ICE CREAM
2 free-range egg yolks
$1/4$ cup sugar
$1/2$ cup water
$1/2$ teaspoon pure vanilla extract
$2^1/2$ cups softly whipped cream
(measurement of cream when
whipped)

KUMQUAT COMPOTE
$3^1/2$ pounds kumquats
I quart water
$2^1/2$ cups sugar

CHOCOLATE DIAMONDS
8 ounces bittersweet or semisweet
chocolate (with a high percentage of
cocoa butter)

DECORATION
Fresh or crystallized mint leaves
(optional)

For a fancy presentation to dazzle the pals at a dinner party: chill the serving plates; let the ice cream soften a little before shaping it into almond shapes, using two spoons or an ice cream scoop; arrange three on their sides in a flower shape on the chilled plates (better still, do this ahead and chill again before finishing); spoon a little compote between the almond shapes of ice cream and arrange a diamond-shaped piece of chocolate on its side in the gaps. Finish with a sprig of fresh or crystallized mint in the center and serve immediately—a delicious combination of flavors. For a less stressful presentation, serve the ice cream and compote simply in chilled bowls and offer the chocolate diamonds separately—equally delicious, but not quite so dramatic.

The quality of cream that has real flavor and the quality of good, fresh free-range eggs are the secret of a good ice cream, as well as, in this instance, a pure vanilla extract.

First make the ice cream. Put the egg yolks into a bowl and whisk until light and fluffy (keep the whites for meringues). Combine the sugar and water in a small heavy saucepan and stir over heat until the sugar is completely dissolved; then remove the spoon and boil the syrup until it reaches the thread stage, 223–236°F. It will look thick and syrupy; when a metal spoon is dipped in, the last drops of syrup will form thin threads. Pour this boiling syrup in a steady stream onto the egg yolks, whisking all the time. Add the vanilla and continue to whisk until it becomes a thick, creamy white mousse. Fold the softly whipped cream into the mousse, pour into a bowl, cover, and freeze for at least 6 hours.

Meanwhile, poach the fruit. Slice each kumquat into four circles and remove the seeds. Put the kumquats into a saucepan with the water and sugar and cover the pan. Let them cook very gently for about half an hour. Cool, then chill in the refrigerator until needed.

Next make the chocolate diamonds. Melt the chocolate in a very low oven or in a heatproof bowl set over barely simmering water. Spread the melted chocolate fairly thickly over a sheet of silicone paper. Leave to get cold and firm before cutting into strips about I inch wide and then into diamonds at an angle.

Decorate with the mint leaves, if using.

Blood Orange Tart

SERVES 8

PASTRY
I¹/₄ cups all-purpose flour
I tablespoon sugar
6 tablespoons butter
About 2 tablespoons orange juice or
water
I free-range egg yolk

FILLING
6 tablespoons butter
¹/₂ cup sugar
I whole free-range egg and
2 free-range egg yolks
I cup ground almonds
I tablespoon Grand Marnier

DECORATION
6 blood oranges

4–6 tablespoons Apricot Glaze
(see page 86)

YOU WILL NEED
A 10-inch tart pan with removable base

Of all the citrus fruits, blood oranges excite me most. They appear in our shops for only about four weeks from the end of January, so we use them in juices and cocktails, fruit salads, tarts, sorbets, granitas, Mimosas...

Preheat the oven to 350°F.

Sift the flour into a bowl and add the sugar. Cut the cold butter into cubes and cut into the dry ingredients until the mixture resembles coarse bread crumbs. Mix the orange juice or water with the egg yolk and use to bind the pastry. Add a little more water if necessary, but don't make it too sticky. Wrap and refrigerate for 30 minutes or so. Roll out the pastry and line the tart pan. Line with parchment paper, fill with ceramic baking beans and bake for 20–25 minutes.

Meanwhile, make the filling. Cream the butter, add the sugar, and beat until light and fluffy. Add the egg and egg yolks and beat well, then stir in the ground almonds and the liqueur.

When the tart shell is part baked, let it cool. Brush the bottom with apricot glaze and fill with the almond mixture. Return to the oven and bake for about 20 minutes or until the almond filling is cooked and firm to the touch, in the center as well as at the sides.

Meanwhile, remove the peel and pith from the blood oranges, then section them. Drain, and arrange in a pattern on top of the warm tart. Alternatively, slice the peeled oranges into thin rounds and arrange, slightly overlapping, on top of the warm tart. This looks prettiest, but is slightly trickier to slice. Either way, paint the oranges evenly with apricot glaze.

Serve warm with a bowl of softly whipped cream.

Marzipan Apple Tart

SERVES 8–10

1 recipe quantity Shortcrust Pastry
(see page 183)

MARZIPAN
1 cup plus 2 tablespoons sugar
5 tablespoons water
2 cups ground almonds
1 drop of pure almond extract
1 free-range egg white

3 apples
1 tablespoon butter, melted
1 teaspoon freshly ground cinnamon
2 tablespoons sugar

YOU WILL NEED
A 9-inch tart pan with removable base

This tart keeps very well.

First make the pastry. Let it rest for 30 minutes in the refrigerator if time allows.

Preheat the oven to 350°F.

Roll out the pastry thinly and line the tart pan. Line with parchment paper and fill the shell with ceramic baking beans. Bake in the preheated oven for 15–20 minutes.

Meanwhile, make the marzipan. Dissolve the sugar in the water and bring to a boil. Cook to 240°F, or the soft ball stage, keeping the sides of the saucepan brushed down with water. Remove from the heat and stir the syrup until cloudy. Add the ground almonds, extract, and slightly beaten egg white. Mix very thoroughly. Pour into the tart shell if ready; alternatively, pour into a bowl and spread in the tart shell later.

Peel the apples, cut into quarters, and core. Slice the apples into $^1/_4$-inch slices and arrange in overlapping circles over the marzipan in the tart shell. Brush lightly with the melted butter. Mix the cinnamon with the sugar and sprinkle over the apples. Bake in the preheated oven for about 35 minutes.

Serve warm or cold, with softly whipped cream.

Walnut Tart with Armagnac

SERVES 8–10

PASTRY
1²/₃ cups all-purpose flour
Pinch of salt
¹/₂ cup (1 stick) butter
¹/₄ cup sugar
2 free-range egg yolks
Few drops of pure vanilla extract
(optional)

WALNUT FILLING
1¹/₂ cups freshly shelled walnuts,
roughly chopped
1¹/₂ cups heavy cream
¹/₂ teaspoon pure vanilla extract
¹/₂ cup plus 1 tablespoon sugar
Pinch of salt
2 medium egg whites

ICING
3 tablespoons Armagnac or Brandy
1¹/₂ cups confectioners' sugar

DECORATION
16 walnut halves

YOU WILL NEED
A 10-inch flan ring or tart pan,
preferably with removable base

Every autumn we buy a sack of walnuts from Mr. Bell in the Cork market—it's a heck of a lot more labor-intensive to have to crack each nut, but it's worth it to be sure of fresh rather than rancid walnuts. Delicious warm or cold, this winter tart keeps for up to a week.

Make the pastry in the usual way. I don't bother with a bowl; I just sift the flour with a pinch of salt onto the clean worktop and make a well in the center with the back of my hand. Cut the butter into small cubes and add with the sugar, egg yolks, and a few drops of vanilla extract, if using. With the fingertips of one hand, work these ingredients together until well mixed (the texture will resemble scrambled eggs), then quickly draw in the flour, running your fingers through the mixture to coat the particles of butter and egg. Form the mixture into a line, then, with the heel of the hand, knead the pastry away from you in quick rhythmic movements. Gather up the dough again and repeat twice more, by which time the pastry should be perfectly amalgamated. Finally, knead lightly to get into a smooth ball. Then roll into a flat round, cover with plastic wrap, and let rest in the refrigerator for 1 hour. If this all sounds too messy, make the pastry in a food processor or a bowl.

Preheat the oven to 350°F.

Roll out the pastry and line the flan ring or tart pan. Line with parchment paper and fill with ceramic baking beans. Bake in the preheated oven for about 10 minutes, then remove the paper and beans and bake for a further 5 minutes or until golden and firm (this pastry must not brown or it will taste bitter).

Meanwhile, make the filling. Mix the walnuts with the cream, vanilla, sugar, and a pinch of salt. When the tart shell is ready, fold the stiffly beaten egg whites into the filling and pour into the baked tart shell. Return the tart to the oven and bake for about 45 minutes or until set and pale golden.

Meanwhile, make the icing: simply mix the Armagnac or brandy with the sifted confectioners' sugar to make thickish icing.

When the tart is cooked, let it cool a little in the flan ring or pan. Then transfer to a wire rack. While still slightly warm, pour the icing over and spread gently and evenly with a small metal spatula. Decorate with walnut halves and serve with a bowl of softly whipped cream.

Agen Prunes with Walnuts and Rosewater Cream

SERVES 6

1 pound Agen prunes or other good
prunes
Same number of fresh walnut halves
About ²/₃ cup each red wine and water,
or 1¹/₄ cups water
1¹/₄ cups heavy cream
2 tablespoons sugar
1 tablespoon rosewater

DECORATION
A few chopped walnuts
Rose petals (optional)

This ancient recipe from the Middle East will change your opinion of prunes—a pretty and delicious dish that tastes even better next day. We have experimented with taking out the spits from both soaked and dry prunes; unsoaked worked best. Claudia Roden originally introduced me to this recipe when she taught at the school.

Use a small knife to cut out the pits from the prunes and then stuff each with half a walnut. Arrange in a single layer in a sauté pan. Cover with a mixture of wine and water. Put the lid on the pan and simmer for about 30 minutes. Add more liquid if they become a little dry. They should be plump and soft. Lift them gently onto a serving plate in a single layer and let them cool.

Whip the cream to soft peaks and add the sugar and rosewater. Spoon blobs over the prunes and chill well. Just before serving, scatter a few chopped walnuts over each blob of cream, sprinkle with rose petals, and serve well chilled.

Focaccia with Caramelized Onions, Cashel Blue Cheese, and Walnuts

SERVES 1–2

FOR THE CARAMELIZED ONIONS
Olive oil
5 onions, thinly sliced

¹/₃ recipe quantity Ballymaloe White Yeast Bread dough (see page 180)—about 14 ounces dough
Semolina or cornmeal

3–4 ounces Cashel Blue cheese
¹/₄–¹/₂ cup roughly chopped walnuts

We make many, many types of bread at Ballymaloe Cookery School. This one can be served as a first course or a nibble, or even, with cheese, as a meal. Make the Ballymaloe White Yeast Bread dough, and use the leftover dough to make crusty rolls. I have used Cashel Blue here, but you can just as well use Stilton or Gorgonzola.

Preheat the oven to 450°F.

First make the caramelized onions. Heat 2-3 tablespoons of olive oil in a heavy saucepan, toss in the onions, and cook on low heat so that they soften slowly and lightly caramelize to a pale golden brown (say 20–30 minutes).

Roll out the dough to a round ¹/₂ inch thick and 12 inches in diameter. Sprinkle some semolina or cornmeal onto a pizza paddle and place the dough on top. Slide onto an oiled baking sheet. Make indentations all over the surface of the dough round with your fingertips. Cover the surface of the dough to within ³/₄ inch of the edge with caramelized onions. Crumble the Cashel Blue cheese and scatter over the top, then sprinkle with chopped walnuts. Drizzle with a little olive oil and bake in the preheated oven for 20 minutes. Serve immediately.

Wheaten Bread

Wheaten breads and soda breads are very fast to make and are still made widely throughout the Irish countryside. Buttermilk is available in every village shop. Flavor varies according to the type of flour, recipe, and, of course, the "turn of hand" of the baker. The traditional loaf is shaped into a round and then scored into quarters. A cross is then made with the tip of a knife—to let the fairies out, so they won't jinx your bread. The fairies are very active in Ireland, particularly around Halloween; none of us to this day would dream of making a loaf of Irish wheaten or soda bread without letting the fairies out. It's part of what we are!

Preheat the oven to 450°F.

MAKES 1 LARGE ROUND LOAF

5 cups whole-wheat flour
(preferably stone-ground)
4 cups all-purpose flour
2 teaspoons salt
2 teaspoons baking soda
3³/₄ cups sour milk or buttermilk

Mix the dry ingredients well together. Make a well in the center and add about 3 cups of the sour milk or buttermilk. Working from the center, mix with your hand and add more milk if necessary. The dough should be soft but not sticky. Turn out onto a floured board; wash and dry your hands and sprinkle them with flour, then tidy the dough just enough to shape into a round. Flatten slightly to about 2 inches thick. Put onto a floured baking sheet. Mark with a deep cross. Bake in the preheated oven for 15–20 minutes, then reduce the temperature to 400°F and continue baking for 20–25 minutes or until the bread is cooked and sounds hollow when tapped on the base. Cool on a wire rack.

Note: You could add 3 tablespoons oatmeal flour, 1 egg, and 2 tablespoons butter to the above to make a richer wheaten dough.

Lovisa's Swedish Flat Bread

MAKES ABOUT 20

2 teaspoons caraway seeds
3 cakes (0.6–ounce each) compressed fresh yeast
2 cups tepid milk
6 cups plain rye flour (sometimes more)
4¹/₂ cups all-purpose flour
2 teaspoons salt
2 cups coarse rye flour (for dusting the board)

YOU WILL NEED
A 1-inch round cookie cutter

I came home from my first trip to Norway in 1995, armed with a spiky rolling pin and the taste memories of many delicious Norwegian foods, including their thin, crisp flat breads. As luck would have it, I had a lovely Swedish girl on my new Certificate course. One day she told me that her mother had just sent her a recipe for the flat bread that she missed so much. Did I have any rye flour, and could she make it at the school? I couldn't believe my luck—and she couldn't believe her eyes when she discovered a Knackebröd rolling pin in Shanagarry! The flat bread is so delicious that we asked for the recipe on the first bite. It will keep for weeks—if you can resist nibbling it constantly.

Preheat the oven to 350°F.

Grind the caraway seeds finely in a mortar and pestle.

Crumble the yeast and pour the tepid milk over it. Mix the flours with the salt and the caraway seeds. Sift the flours into the liquid and stir with a wooden spoon. Gather the dough together and turn onto a floured board. Shape the dough into a thick rope and divide into 20 pieces. Knead the pieces into balls, then cover and let rise for 20 minutes.

Sprinkle the coarse rye flour on the board. Roll out each ball with a smooth rolling pin and then roll with the spiky rolling pin. (Alternatively, prick each flat bread with a fork.)

Turn the dough to keep the round shape and roll out to 8 inches in diameter. Lovisa stamps out a little hole in the center of each flat bread in the traditional way using a 1-inch cutter.

Bake on a lightly greased baking sheet in the preheated oven for 8–10 minutes. Cool on a wire rack. Eat warm or cold.

Ballymaloe White Yeast Bread

MAKES 2 1-POUND LOAVES

1 cake (0.6-ounce) fresh yeast
2 tablespoons butter
2 teaspoons salt
1¹/₂ tablespoons sugar
6 cups white bread flour
Egg wash, or 1 free-range egg yolk and
2 tablespoons cream beaten together
Poppy or sesame seeds (optional)

YOU WILL NEED

2 loaf pans, measuring 8¹/₂ by 4¹/₂ by
2¹/₂ inches, brushed with
non-scented oil

We make this dough into braids, use it as the base for pizzas (substitute olive oil for the butter), and shape it into rolls and loaves.

Mix the yeast with ²/₃ cup of lukewarm water until it dissolves. Put the butter, salt, and sugar into a bowl with ²/₃ cup of very hot water and stir until the sugar and salt are dissolved and the butter has melted. Add ²/₃ cup of cold water. By now, the liquid should be lukewarm or at blood heat, so combine with the yeast.

Sift the flour into a bowl, make a well in the center, and pour in most of the lukewarm liquid. Mix to a loose dough, adding the remaining liquid; add more flour or water if necessary. Turn the dough onto a floured board, cover, and let relax for 5–10 minutes. Then knead vigorously for about 10 minutes or until smooth and springy (if kneading in an electric mixer with a dough hook, 5 minutes is usually long enough).

Put the dough to rise in a pottery bowl and cover tightly with plastic wrap. Yeast dough rises best in a warm, moist atmosphere: near your stove or on top of a radiator is a good spot. However, if your kitchen is warm enough for you, the bread will rise in its own time, about 2–3 hours.

When the dough has more than doubled in size, knead again for 2–3 minutes until all the air has been forced out—this is called punching down. Let the dough relax again for 10 minutes.

Preheat the oven to 450°F.

Shape the bread into loaves, braids, or rolls, sprinkle with poppy or sesame seeds, if you desire, and cover with a light dish towel. Let rise again in a warm place; this rising will be much shorter (only 20–30 minutes). The dough is ready for baking if a small dent remains when the dough is pressed lightly with a finger. Brush with egg wash, egg and cream glaze or water.

Bake in the preheated oven for 30–35 minutes. Remove from the pans about 10 minutes before the end of baking and return to the oven to bake the crust underneath. Cool on a wire rack.

White Soda Bread

MAKES 1 BIG LOAF

3 cups unbleached all-purpose flour
1 teaspoon salt
1 teaspoon baking soda
1¹/₂ cups sour milk or buttermilk to mix

Soda bread only takes 2–3 minutes to make and 20–30 minutes to bake. It is certainly another of my great "convertibles." We have had the greatest fun experimenting with different variations and uses. This kind of bread is also great with olives, sun-dried tomatoes, or caramelized onions added, so the possibilities are endless for the hitherto humble soda bread.

Preheat the oven to 450°F.

Sift the dry ingredients into a bowl and make a well in the center. Pour in most of the milk at once. Using one hand, mix in the flour from the sides of the bowl, adding more milk if necessary. The dough should be softish, not too wet and sticky. When it all comes together, turn it out onto a floured board and knead lightly for a second, just enough to tidy it up. Pat the dough into a round about 1 inch thick and cut a cross on it to let the fairies out! Let the cuts go over the sides of the bread to make sure of this. Bake in the preheated oven for 20 minutes, then turn the temperature down to 400°F and continue baking for 15 minutes or until cooked. If you are in doubt, tap the base of the bread: if it is cooked, it will sound hollow.

White Soda Scones

Make the dough as above, flattening the dough into a round about 1 inch thick, and then cut into scones. Bake for about 20 minutes in a hot oven (see above).

White Soda Bread with Herbs

Add 2 tablespoons of freshly chopped herbs, such as rosemary, sage, thyme, chives, parsley, and lemon balm, to the dry ingredients. Shape into a loaf or scones and bake.

Basic recipes

In this section we've gathered together all the miscellaneous recipes referred to in the main chapters of the book.

Ballymaloe Vinaigrette

Never swamp salads with dressing: use just enough to make the greens glisten. Green salads must not be dressed until just before serving, otherwise they become tired and unappetizing.

$1/4$ cup wine vinegar
$3/4$ cup olive oil (or a mixture of olive and either sunflower or peanut oils)
1 teaspoon mustard (Dijon or prepared English)
1 large clove garlic
1 scallion
Sprig of parsley
Sprig of watercress
1 teaspoon salt
Few grinds of black pepper

Put all the ingredients into a blender and work at medium speed for about 1 minute. Or, mix the oil and vinegar in a bowl and add the mustard, salt, freshly ground pepper and minced garlic. Mince the parsley, scallion and watercress and add. Whisk before using.

Grainy Mustard Sauce

Quick to make and delicious with pork.

1 cup heavy cream
2 teaspoons mild brown mustard
1 tablespoon whole-grain mustard
Salt and freshly ground black pepper

Put the cream and both mustards in a small pan and bring slowly to a boil, stirring occasionally. Taste and season if necessary.

Roux

Roux can be stored in a cool place (up to two weeks in a refrigerator), or made up as and when required. Whisk into boiling liquid to thicken sauces, gravies, stews, etc.
$1/2$ cup (1 stick) butter
$3/4$ cup all-purpose flour

Melt the butter and cook the flour in it for 2 minutes on low heat, stirring occasionally.

Béchamel Sauce

This is a wonderfully quick way of making Béchamel Sauce if you have Roux already made.

MAKES $1 1/4$ CUPS

$1 1/2$ cups milk
A few slices of carrot
A few slices of onion
3 black peppercorns
Small sprig of fresh thyme
Small sprig of parsley
3 tablespoons Roux (see page 185)
Salt and freshly ground black pepper

Put the cold milk into a saucepan with the carrot, onion, peppercorns, thyme, and parsley. Bring to a boil and simmer for 4–5 minutes then remove from the heat and let infuse for 10 minutes. Strain out the vegetables. Bring the milk back to a boil and thicken to a light coating consistency by whisking in the roux. Add salt and pepper to taste.

Hollandaise Sauce

Delicious with asparagus or fish.

2 egg yolks, preferably free-range
$1/2$ cup (1 stick) butter, cut into dice
2 teaspoons cold water
About 1 teaspoon lemon juice

Put the egg yolks into a heavy-bottomed stainless-steel pan on very low heat. Add the cold water and thoroughly whisk. Gradually add the cubed butter—as one piece melts, add the next—whisking all the time. The mixture will gradually thicken; if it begins to "scramble" or become too thick, remove from the heat; add a little more cold water if necessary. Do not stop whisking until the sauce is complete. Finally, add the lemon juice to taste. Pour into a bowl and keep warm over a pan of hot but not boiling water.

Tomato Fondue

Tomato Fondue is one of our great convertibles. It has a number of uses—we serve it as a vegetable, sauce, filling for omelettes, topping for pizza, stuffing, and so on. Cook it quickly for a fresh taste or slowly for a stronger taste, particularly if you are using canned tomatoes. It is great with added hot green chile peppers. We often toss green beans in it.

SERVES ABOUT 6

1 tablespoon olive oil
$3/4$ cup sliced onions
1 clove garlic, minced
2 pounds very ripe tomatoes, peeled, in summer, or 4 cups canned tomatoes in winter
Salt and freshly ground black pepper
Sugar
About 1 tablespoon chopped fresh mint or torn basil,

Heat the oil in a non-metal saucepan. Add the sliced onions and garlic, toss until coated, and cook, covered, on low heat until soft. It is vital for the success of this dish that the onions are completely soft before the tomatoes are added. Slice the tomatoes and add to the pan with all the juices. Season with salt, pepper, and sugar (canned tomatoes need lots of sugar because of their high acidity). Add a generous sprinkling of chopped mint or torn basil. Cook, uncovered, for 10–20 more minutes, or until the tomato softens.

Vine-Ripened Tomato Purée

Tomato Purée is one of the very best ways of preserving the flavor of ripe summer tomatoes for winter, to use in soups, stews, and casseroles. We make heaps of it at the end of August, when we have a glut of tomatoes that burst with flavor. Make lots and freeze it to help you through the winter.

2 pounds vine-ripened tomatoes
1 small onion, chopped
Large pinch of salt
A few twists of black pepper
2 teaspoons sugar

Cut the very ripe tomatoes into quarters and put into a stainless steel saucepan with the onion, salt, pepper, and sugar. Cook on low heat until the tomatoes are soft (no water is needed). Put through the fine blade of a vegetable mill or a nylon strainer.

Leave to get cold, then refrigerate or freeze.

Puff Pastry

Homemade puff pastry takes a little time to make, but it is more than worth the effort for its wonderful flavor, which bears no relation to the commercial equivalent. It is essential to use butter!

MAKES ABOUT 2 POUNDS 10 OUNCES

4 cups white bread flour, chilled
Pinch of salt
Squeeze of lemon juice (optional)
$1^1/4$-$1^1/2$ cups cold water
2 cups (4 sticks) butter, firm but pliable

Sift the chilled flour and salt into a bowl and mix to a firm dough with water and a squeeze of lemon juice if liked. This dough is called *détrempe*. Cover with wax paper or plastic wrap and let rest for 30 minutes in the refrigerator.

Roll the *détrempe* into a square about $1/2$ inch thick. If the butter is very hard, beat it (still in its wrapper) with a rolling pin until pliable but not sticky. Unwrap the butter and shape into a slab roughly about $3/4$ inch thick. Place in the center of the dough and fold the dough over the edges of the butter to make a neat parcel. Make sure your chilled marble pastry board is well floured, then flatten the dough with a rolling pin and continue to roll out into a rectangle about 18 inches long and 6 inches wide (these measurements are only approximate, so don't be too particular!). Fold neatly into thirds to make an oblong with the edges as accurately aligned as possible. Seal the edges with a rolling pin.

Give the dough a quarter turn (90°): it should now be on your pastry board as though it was a book with the length of it pointing away from you. Roll out again, fold in thirds, and seal the edges with the rolling pin. Cover with plastic wrap or wax paper and let rest in the refrigerator for at least 30 minutes before use.

Shortcrust Pastry

MAKES ENOUGH TO LINE A 9-INCH
DIAMETER FLAN RING

$1^1/2$ cups all-purpose flour
2 teaspoons sugar
$1/2$ cup (1 stick) cold butter
1 egg yolk, preferably free-range
3–4 tablespoons cold water

Sift the flour and sugar into a bowl. Cut the butter into cubes and cut into the flour. Keep everything as cool as possible: if the fat is allowed to melt, the finished pastry may be tough. When the mixture looks like coarse bread crumbs, stop mixing.

Whisk the egg yolk and add the water.

Take a fork or knife and mix in just enough liquid to bring the pastry together. Discard the fork and collect the pastry into a ball with your hands. This way you can judge more accurately if you need a few more drops of egg liquid. Although slightly damp pastry is easier to handle and roll out, the resulting crust can be tough and may well shrink out of shape as the water evaporates in the oven. Drier (and more difficult-to-handle) pastry will give a crisper, shorter crust.

Cover the pastry with plastic wrap and let rest in the refrigerator for a minimum of 15 minutes, or, better still, 30 minutes. This will make the pastry much less elastic and easier to roll.

Polenta

Polenta can be served the moment it is cooked, or it can be turned into a rinsed dish and left to get cold. It can then be sliced and chargrilled, pangrilled, toasted, or fried, and served with all sorts of toppings. It can even be cut into thin slices and layered with a sauce, just like lasagne.

SERVES 6–8

$7^1/2$ cups water
2 teaspoons salt
2 cups coarse polenta flour (cornmeal)
$1/2$ cup (1 stick) butter
$3/4$-1 cup freshly grated
     Parmesan cheese (Parmigiano Reggiano is
     best) (optional)
Sea salt and freshly ground black pepper

Put the water into a deep, heavy saucepan and bring to a boil. Add the salt, then sprinkle in the polenta flour very slowly, letting it slip gradually through your fingers, whisking all the time (this should take 3–4 minutes). Bring to a boil again and when it starts to "erupt like a volcano," turn the heat down to the absolute minimum—use a flame tamer if you have one. Cook for about 40 minutes, stirring regularly (I use a whisk at the beginning, but as soon as the polenta comes to a boil I change to a flat wooden spoon). If you stir constantly on a slightly higher heat, the cooking time can be reduced to about 20 minutes, but polenta is more digestible if cooked more slowly over a longer period. The polenta is cooked when it is very thick but not solid and comes away from the sides of the pan as you stir.

As soon as the polenta is cooked, stir in the butter, freshly grated Parmesan, and lots of pepper. Taste and add a little more sea salt if necessary. The polenta should be soft and flowing; if it is a little too stiff, add some boiling water.

Serve immediately. Try it with Sweet-Sour Pork with Prunes, Raisins, and Pine Nuts (see page 160).

Flavored Oils and Vinegars

Herbs are at their most aromatic just before they flower. So in June and July, we make our stock of infused oils and vinegars for the year. We started years ago with basil oil, when basil was rare and scarce—it was a way of preserving every last precious leaf. This led to experiments with other herbs, such as rosemary, annual marjoram, oregano, thyme leaves, and sage. Some herbs, including tarragon and dill, preserve better in vinegar; we have also had success with elderflower vinegar. Fruit vinegars work well, too, but we make very little because in practice we used very small quantities after the initial novelty had worn off.

Herb oils and vinegars we use in abundance, and discover more uses all the time. Chile oil, roasted garlic oil, and dried mushroom oil have also become standard drizzles for everything from flavoring croûtons to pasta, salads, soups, and mashed potatoes, or just an addictive dipping oil for crusty bread.

In general, we are not very scientific in the way we make our flavored oil. We simply pour out a little oil from the bottle (in most cases, I use extra virgin olive oil—Lesieur or Puget are the brands we use large quantities of at present) and stuff the herbs down into the oil. The quantity varies depending on whether one wants a mild or strong flavor—experiment.

I am sure it would be more correct to wash and dry the herbs carefully, but I have to say that I rarely do because our herbs come straight into the kitchen from the garden or greenhouse. We top up the bottles with oil and replace the lid tightly. I store basil oil in the refrigerator or cold room, but the other oils sit on a shelf in the pantry and kitchens. They are best left to infuse for a few days and then used within a few weeks.

Basil Oil

The basil can be used either to flavor the oil or the oil can be used to preserve the basil, depending on the quantity.

Olive oil
Fresh basil leaves

Check the basil leaves and make sure that they are clean and dry. Pour a little of the olive oil out of the bottle, stuff at least 8–10 basil leaves into the bottle, and top up with oil. Seal and store in a cold place.

Chile Oil (Olio Picante)

Stuff 1–6 dried hot chile peppers down into a bottle of oil, top up, and let infuse for a few days before using.

Chile, Herb, and Pepper Oil

One of my favorite combinations is 1–2 hot chile peppers, a sprig or two of fresh rosemary or annual marjoram, and a teaspoon of black peppercorns. This is particularly good for brushing over steaks, lamb chops, or chicken breasts to be chargrilled.

Roasted Garlic Oil

The oil used to roast garlic (see page 83) is great stuff for cooking croûtons or crostini, or for drizzling over salads, into soups, vegetable stews, pasta, and so on. Make in small quantities and use within a week because it can ferment.

Crostini

Crostini are very good made into Tapenade Toasts (see page 186).

Put 1 inch of olive oil in a skillet and heat until very hot. Sauté the slices of French bread, one at a time, turning as soon as they are golden. Drain on paper towels.

Extra virgin olive oil for frying
8–10 $^1/_4$-inch thick slices French
    bread or ciabatta, cut at an angle

Homemade Chicken Stock

Instead of absent-mindedly throwing them away, keep your poultry carcasses and giblets and vegetable trimmings, and use them for your stockpot. Nowadays some supermarkets and poulterers are happy to give you chicken carcasses or giblets, because there is so little demand for them.

MAKES ABOUT 3$^1/_2$ QUARTS

2–3 raw or cooked carcasses, or both
    Chicken giblets—neck, heart, gizzard
About 3$^1/_2$ quarts water
I onion, sliced
I leek, split in two
I outside stalk of celery or I lovage leaf
I carrot, sliced
A few parsley stems
Sprig of fresh thyme
6 black peppercorns

Chop up the carcasses as much as possible. Put all the ingredients into a large pot. Bring to a boil and skim the fat off the top with a metal spoon. Simmer for 3–5 hours. Strain and remove any remaining fat. If you need a stronger flavor, boil the liquid in an open pan to reduce by one-third or one-half of the volume. Do not add salt.

Note: Stock will keep for several days in the refrigerator. If you want to keep it longer, boil it up again for 5–6 minutes every day, then cool it quickly and refrigerate again. Stock also freezes perfectly. For cheap containers use large yogurt cartons; then you can cut them off without pricking your concience if you are in a hurry! In restaurants, stock is usually allowed to simmer uncovered so it will be as clear as possible, but I usually advise people making stock at home to cover the pot, otherwise the whole house will smell of stock.

This recipe is just a guideline. If you have just one carcass and cannot be bothered to make a small quantitiy of stock, save it in the freezer until you have 3 or 4 carcasses and giblets. Then you can make a really good sized pot of stock.

Don't use chicken livers because they will make your stock bitter. There are also some vegetables that should not be put in the stockpot: potatoes soak up the flavor and make the stock cloudy; parsnips are too strong, as are beets; cabbage and other crucifers can give out an "off-taste" after they have been cooked for a while. A little turnip is sometimes an asset, but it is very easy to overdo it. I also ban bay leaf in my chicken stocks because I find that the flavor of bay can easily predominate and add a sameness to all soups made from that stock.

Salt is another ingredient that has no place in my stocks. This is because salted stocks can easily become oversalted when they are reduced to make sauces.

Homemade Duck Stock

This makes a simple stock and can be used as the basis of duck gravy.

Duck neck, gizzard, heart and any other
    trimmings
I medium carrot, sliced
I onion, quartered
Bouquet garni of parsley stalks, celery
    stalk, and thyme sprig
2 or 3 peppercorns

Follow the instructions for the Chicken Stock recipe (see page 184). Cover all the ingredients in a saucepan with cold water, bring slowly to the boil and simmer for 2–3 hours.

Basic Chinese Stock

This delicious stock forms the essential base of many delicious light fish or meat soups. Equal quantities of chicken pieces and spare ribs can be used, or 4 pounds of either. The stock will keep in the refrigerator for several days; after that, boil it every 2 or 3 days. It also freezes perfectly.

MAKES ABOUT 2 QUARTS

2 pounds chicken giblets, wings, necks,
    hearts, gizzards, etc.
2 pounds pork spare ribs
$I^1/_2$-inch piece fresh ginger root,
    unpeeled, thinly sliced
6 large scallions
$4^1/_2$–$5^1/_2$ quarts Homemade Chicken Stock
    (see page 184)
4 tablespoons Shao Hsing rice wine

Put all the ingredients, except the rice wine, in a large saucepan. Bring to a boil and skim off any scum. Reduce the heat, cover, and simmer gently for about 4 hours, skimming regularly. Add the rice wine 5 minutes before the end of the cooking time. Strain the stock and let cool, then refrigerate.

Remove the solidified fat from the top of the stock before use.

Homemade Vegetable Stock

This is just a rough guide—you can make a vegetable stock from any available vegetable, but try not to use too much of any one unless you particularly want that flavor to predominate. This stock keeps for a week in a refrigerator.

MAKES $2^1/_2$ QUARTS

I small turnip
2 onions, roughly sliced, or the green parts
    of 2–3 leeks
3 stalks celery, roughly chopped
3 large carrots, roughly chopped
$^1/_2$ Florence fennel bulb, roughly chopped
2 medium-sized potatoes, scrubbed and
    roughly chopped
4–6 parsley stems
$2^1/_2$ quarts cold water
Bouquet garni
$I^1/_2$ cups sliced mushrooms
A few black peppercorns

Put all the ingredients into a large saucepan and bring to a boil. Turn the heat down, cover the pan, and let simmer for $I^1/_2$–2 hours. Strain.

Homemade Beef Stock

Brown beef stock is used for beef and game stews and for sauces. This stock will keep for 2–3 days in the refrigerator. If you want to keep it for longer, boil it for 10 minutes, and then refrigerate again. It can also be frozen.

MAKES 4 QUARTS

5–6 pounds beef bones,
    preferably with some scraps of meat
    on, sawed into small pieces
2 large onions, quartered
2 large carrots, quartered
3 stems celery, cut into 1-inch pieces
Large bouquet garni (parsley stems, bay
    leaf, fresh thyme and tarragon)
10 black peppercorns
2 whole cloves
4 cloves garlic, unpeeled
I teaspoon tomato paste
4 quarts water

Preheat the oven to 450°F.

Put the bones into a roasting pan and roast for 30 minutes or until the bones are well browned. Add the onions, carrots, and celery and return to the oven to roast until the vegetables are also browned. Transfer the bones and vegetables to the stockpot with a metal spoon. Add the bouquet garni, peppercorns, cloves, garlic, and tomato paste. Skim the fat from the roasting pan and deglaze with some of the water. Bring to a boil and pour over the bones and vegetables. Add the remaining water and bring to a boil slowly. Skim the stock, then let simmer gently for 5–6 hours. Strain the stock, let it get cold, and skim off all the fat before use.

Pesto

Pesto is one of the new basics. It is extremely easy to make if you can get hold of any herbs. Even better, grow your own, as basil is so expensive. We grow so much basil. It really starts to grow in summer, and you must pick it before the flowers blossom. The term pesto is becoming more and more elastic. Use culinary license and experiment with new combinations—we love tomato and mint! Try using different herbs, olives, and sun-dried tomatoes.

Pesto keeps for weeks in the refrigerator in a sterilized jar, covered with a generous layer of olive oil, in the refridgerator. Always use a clean spoon! It also freezes well, but for best results don't add the grated Parmesan until it has defrosted. Eat it with pastas, or drizzle it over fish or chargrilled chicken. It really jazzes up a tomato salad in the winter.

$2^1/2$ cups fresh basil leaves
$2/3$ cup extra virgin olive oil
$1/4$ cup fresh pine nuts (taste one to make sure they are not rancid)
2 large cloves garlic, peeled and minced
$1/2$ cups freshly and finely grated Parmesan cheese (preferably Parmigiano Reggiano)
Salt

In a food processor, whizz the basil with the olive oil, pine nuts and garlic, or pound them in a mortar and pestle. Remove to a bowl and fold in the Parmesan cheese. Taste and season with salt.

Variations
Mint and Parsley Pesto

Substitute $1^1/4$ cups each of fresh mint and fresh parsley for the basil in the above recipe.

Parsley Pesto

If you do not have any basil, then parsley pesto is a good alternative. We make it throughout the winter, often enlivening it with some chile. It is marvelous drizzled over roasted vegetables, fish, or pangrilled chicken. You may want to alter the proportion of olive oil.

2 cups flat-leaf parsley (no stems)
1–2 cloves garlic, peeled and minced
6 tablespoons freshly grated Parmesan cheese (Parmigiano Reggiano is best)
$1/4$ cup pine nuts
$1/3$–$2/3$ cup extra virgin olive oil
Salt

Put all the ingredients, except the oil and salt, into a food processor. Process for a second or two, then add the oil and a little salt. Taste to check the seasoning.

Tapenade

You can buy the olives whole for this recipe, and remove the pits yourself. You will need about 1 cup of unpitted olives. Serve on Crostini (see page 184) as Tapenade Toasts.

SERVES 6–8

A 2-ounce can anchovy fillets
1 cup pitted black Kalamata olives
1 tablespoon capers
1 teaspoon Dijon mustard
1 teaspoon freshly squeezed lemon juice
Freshly ground pepper
2–3 tablespoons extra virgin olive oil

Combine the anchovy fillets, olives, capers, mustard, lemon juice and freshly ground pepper in a food processor and process for just a few seconds. Alternatively, use a mortar andpestle. When it becomes a coarse purée, slowly add the olive oil.

Horseradish Sauce

Horseradish grows wild in many parts of North America, and looks like giant dock leaves. The roots, which you grate, can be dug up at any time of the year. If you cannot find any near you, plant some in your own garden, but be careful because it spreads like mad and can become a pest. This is a fairly mild horseradish sauce. If you want to really clear the sinuses, increase the amount of horseradish.

SERVES 6–8

$1^1/2$–3 tablespoons peeled and grated fresh horseradish root
2 teaspoons wine vinegar
1 teaspoon lemon juice
$1/4$ teaspoon Dijon mustard
$1/4$ teaspoon salt
Pinch of freshly ground black pepper
1 teaspoon sugar
1 cup heavy cream, softly whipped

Put the grated horseradish into a bowl with the vinegar, lemon juice, mustard, salt, pepper, and sugar. Fold in the softly whipped cream, but do not overmix or the sauce will curdle. It keeps for 2–3 days, but cover it tightly so that it does not pick up other flavors in the refrigerator.

Mustard and Horseradish Mayonnaise

SERVES 6–8

2 free-range egg yolks
2 tablespoons Dijon mustard
1 tablespoon sugar
2 tablespoons wine vinegar
$2/3$ cup light olive oil or sunflower oil
1 tablespoon fresh horseradish, grated
1 heaping teaspoon fresh chopped parsley
1 heaping teaspoon fresh chopped tarragon

Put the eggs into a bowl, add the mustard, sugar, and wine vinegar, and mix well. Whisk in the oil gradually as if you were making mayonnaise. Finally, add the horseradish, parsley, and tarragon. Taste and correct the seasoning if necessary. Serve with Carpaccio (see page 23) or smoked trout.

Sweet Dill Mayonnaise

1 extra large egg yolk, preferably free-range
2 tablespoons Dijon mustard
1 tablespoon sugar
$2/3$ cup peanut or sunflower oil
1 tablespoon white wine vinegar
1 tablespoon minced fresh dill
Salt and freshly ground black pepper

Whisk the egg yolk with the mustard and sugar. Add the oil drop by drop, whisking all the time, then add the vinegar and fresh dill. Season to taste.

Pickled Cucumbers

SERVES 8–12

$3^1/_3$ cups thinly sliced English
   cucumber, unpeeled
I medium onion, thinly sliced
$^3/_4$ cup sugar
I tablespoon salt
I cup cider vinegar
I teaspoon mustard seed

Combine the cucumber and onion in a large
bowl. Mix the sugar, salt, vinegar, and mustard
seed together and pour over the vegetables. Place
in a tightly covered container in the refrigerator
and leave for at least 4–5 hours or overnight
before using.

This pickle keeps well for up to a week in the
refrigerator.

Red-Currant Sauce

Serve this with guinea fowl, chicken, turkey, ham
and coarse pâtés.

SERVES 4–6

$^3/_4$ cup sugar
$^1/_2$ cup water
I heaping cup redcurrants

Put the sugar and water into a saucepan and stir
until the sugar dissolves, then bring to a boil.
Toss in the redcurrants, bring back to a boil, and
cook, uncovered, for 4–5 minutes or until the
red-currants burst. Serve hot or cold.

Applesauce

I pound apples (suitable of sauce)
2–4 teaspoons water
About $^1/_3$ cup sugar, depending on the tartness
   of the apples

Peel, quarter, and core the apples. Cut the quarters in half and put in a stainless-steel or cast-iron
pan with the sugar and water. Cover and cook
over low heat until the apples have broken down.
Stir and taste for sweetness, adding a little more
sugar if necessary.

Tomato and Cilantro Salsa (Salsa Cruda)

This fresh sauce is ever present on Mexican
tables.

SERVES 4–6

2 very ripe tomatoes, chopped
I tablespoon chopped onion
I clove garlic, minced
$^1/_2$ –I hot chile pepper, minced
I–2 tablespoons fresh chopped cilantro
Freshly squeezed lime juice
Salt and freshly ground black pepper
Sugar

Mix all the ingredients together. Season with
salt, pepper, and sugar.

Italian Salsa Verde

SERVES 6–8

2 bunches flat-leaf parsley, stems removed
Grated zest and juice of I–2 lemons
3 cloves garlic, minced
2 teaspoons freshly grated horseradish
2 tablespoons salted capers, rinsed
Extra virgin olive oil
Salt and freshly ground black pepper

Put the parsley leaves, lemon zest, garlic,
horseradish, and capers in a food processor.
Process in an on/off method until the mixture is
finely chopped. (Alternatively, chop on a wooden
board with a knife or mezzaluna.) Add the
freshly squeezed lemon juice and enough olive oil
to make a moist sauce. Season to taste with salt
and pepper.

Guacamole

One of my most treasured possessions is a dark
green pottery bowl with a coarse-textured
interior—it was made in the Oaxacan valley in
Mexico for preparing guacamole. I carried it, and
the lava rock pestle, the whole way home as hand
luggage, and have enormously enjoyed using it
ever since. Serve guacamole with Quesadillas,
tortilla chips and hamburgers (see page 124).
This in true Mexican style has no tomato in it.
In Mexico the texture of guacamole differs from
place to place – experiment until you find one
you're happy with. And do look out for Mexican
avocados, if you can find them you will
appreciate the difference.

SERVES 2–4

I ripe avocado, preferably Mexican
I clove garlic, minced
I–2 tablespoons freshly squeezed lime or
   (as a last resort) lemon juice
About I tablespoon olive oil (optional)
I tablespoon fresh coarsely chopped cilantro
Sea salt and freshly ground black pepper

Mash the flesh from the avocado with a fork or,
in a mortar and pestle, with the garlic. Add the
freshly squeezed lime juice, a little olive oil,
cilantro, and salt and pepper to taste.

Mint Sauce

Traditional mint sauce, made with tender young shoots of fresh mint, takes only minutes to make. It is the perfect accompaniment to spring lamb. We are on tenterhooks at Easter, waiting for the first sprigs of mint to eat with the lamb. For those who are expecting a bright green jelly, the slightly dull color and watery texture comes as a surprise. This is how it ought to be. Try it.
MAKES $3/4$ CUP

2 tablespoons minced fresh mint
2 tablespoons sugar
6–8 tablespoons boiling water
2 tablespoons white wine vinegar or
    freshly squeezed lemon juice

Put the mint and sugar into a sauce-boat. Add the boiling water and vinegar or lemon juice. Let infuse for 5–10 minutes before serving.

Serve with Easter Lamb with Roasted Scallions (see page 35).

Crispy Onions

These taste best when freshly cooked, but they may also be cooked in advance.

1 large onion
Milk
Well-seasoned all-purpose flour
Sunflower oil for frying

Peel and slice the onion into $1/4$-inch rings. Separate the rings and cover with milk until needed. Heat the oil in a frying pan to 350°F. Toss the onion rings a few at a time in seasoned flour. Deep-fry until golden in the hot oil. Spread them out on paper towels in a single layer and allow to get cold. (They are delicious: you'll need to hide them or they may disappear!) Just before serving, pop them into a hot oven, uncovered, for just a few minutes.

Parmesan Chips

$1/2$ cup freshly and finely grated Parmesan
    cheese (Parmigiano Reggiano is best)

Preheat the oven to 350°F/gas mark 4.

Line a baking sheet with parchment paper. Draw circles on the paper, either eight 5-inch circles or five $1 1/2$-inch circles. Or draw rectangles.

Carefully fill the marked-out shapes with grated Parmesan. Spread the cheese in an even layer to the edges of the circles or rectangles. Bake in the preheated oven for 15–20 minutes or until golden and bubbling. Remove from the oven and let to cool on the sheet.

The chips can be molded into shapes just before they become cold: drape them over a rolling pin. These are best eaten fresh, but they can be stored in an airtight box.

Sweet Geranium Jelly

We have a collection of sweetly scented geraniums growing on the dining-room window sills: each plant has its own perfume and flavour. Of all the different varieties, *Pelargonium graveolens* is the one we use most in the kitchen, and its haunting flavour is particularly successful in this jelly.

MAKES $6 1/2$ POUNDS

6 pounds cooking apples (we use Bramley
    Seedlings or a mixture of these and crab
    apples)
$9 1/2$ cups water
6–8 large sweet geranium leaves
    (*Pelargonium graveolens*)
2 lemons
Sugar

6–7 sweet geranium leaves

Wash the apples and cut into quarters, but do not remove either the peel or the core. Windfalls may be used, but be sure to cut out the bruised parts. Put the apples into a large saucepan with the water, the geranium leaves, and the thinly pared zest of the lemons. Cook over a medium heat until the apples have dissolved into a pulp – this takes about 30 minutes. Turn the pulp into a jelly bag and let drip until all the juice has come through—usually overnight.

Preheat the oven to 325°F.

Measure the juice into a preserving kettle and allow $2 1/4$ cups sugar to each $2 1/2$ cups of juice. Warm the sugar in the low oven. Squeeze the lemons, strain the juice, and add it to the preserving kettle. Bring to a boil and add the warm sugar. Meanwhile turn up the heat of the oven to 400°F.

Stir the mixture in the preserving kettle over a high heat until the sugar has dissolved. Then boil rapidly without stirring for about 8–10 minutes. In the meantime, sterilize the jars in the preheated hot oven for about 10 minutes.

To test for doneness, put a little jelly onto a chilled plate and cool for a minute or two, then press with your finger: if the jelly wrinkles slightly, it will set. Alternatively, use a sugar thermometer to test for setting point. The jelly will set when the thermometer registers 220°F (at 1000 feet above sealevel).

Skim the jelly, put a geranium leaf into the sterilized jar and fill each one with hot jelly. Cover and seal immediately. Label and store in a cool, dark, dry place.

Variations on Geranium Jelly

Clove Jelly

Add 3–6 whole cloves to the apples as they
stew and put a clove in each jar. Serve on bread
or scones.

Mint Jelly

Add 4–6 large sprigs of fresh mint to the apples
while they are stewing, and add 3–4 tablespoons of minced fresh mint to the jelly just
before it is ladled into jars. Serve with lamb.

Rosemary Jelly

Add two sprigs of fresh rosemary to the apples
as they stew, and put a tiny sprig into each jar.
Serve with lamb.

Candied Julienne of Lemon Peel

This candied peel can be stored in an airtight
container for many weeks. Use it for decorating
cakes and the lemon ice cream on page 44.

2 lemons
Stock syrup: 1 cup sugar and $^3/4$ cup water,
    boiled together for 2 minutes

Peel the lemons very thinly with a swivel top
peeler, being careful not to include the white
pith. Cut the strips into fine julienne. Put in a
saucepan with 2 cups of cold water and simmer
for 5 minutes. Drain, refresh in cold water, and
repeat the process. Put the julienne in a saucepan
with the syrup and cook gently until the peel
looks translucent or opaque. Remove with a
slotted spoon and let cool on parchment paper
or a wire rack. When cold, sprinkle with sugar.

Chocolate Caraque

4 ounces semisweet chocolate

Melt the chocolate and spread it thinly with a
metal spatula on a marble slab. Let it set almost
completely, then, using a sharp knife or clean
paint scraper, shave off long, thin scrolls. Use a
slight sawing action and keep your hand upright.
This is fun to do, but there's quite a lot of skill
involved. You'll get good at it with practise, and
you can always eat the rejects!

(ABOVE) Sweet Geranium Jelly. Of all the different
varieties of geranium we have at Ballymaloe Cookery
School, Pelargonium graveolens is the one we use
most in the kitchen. Its haunting flavour is particularly successful in this jelly.

Index

Aïoli: deep-fried sprats with aïoli 24

Almonds: almond cake with crystallized violets and angelica 48

semifreddo di Mandorle 43

Apples: apple bread and butter pudding 46

applesauce 187

baked Crimson Bramleys with brown sugar and cream 134

black pudding with glazed apples and grainy mustard sauce 154

celery root and apple purée 168

glazed 154

marzipan apple tart 175

Apricot tart 86

Artichoke see Chinese, Globe, Jerusalem

Arugula: carpaccio with slivers of Parmesan, arugula, and truffle oil 23

papardelle with roasted pumpkin, pine nuts, and arugula 124

spiced eggplant with goat cheese and arugula leaves 112

Asparagus: asparagus on buttered toast 27

Hollandaise sauce 182

risotto with fava beans, green peas, asparagus, and sugar snaps 36

sea bass with asparagus and fennel 30

Avocados: guacamole 187

Quesadillas with squash blossoms, mozzarella, guacamole, and tomato salsa 62

Basil: dressing 80

garden herb and herb flower salad with basil dressing and Parmesan chips 80

oil 184

pattypan squash with basil 127

pesto 186

roasted sea bass with roasted cherry tomatoes and basil oil 71

stuffed zucchini blossoms with goat cheese, basil, pesto, and tomato fondue 64

Beans: blackeyed peas and chickpea stew 160

spiced chick-pea soup 148

winter vegetable and bean soup with spicy sausage 149

Beef: baby beef scalopine and spinach with raisins and pine nuts 73

carpaccio with slivers of Parmesan, arugula, and truffle oil 23

chargrilled sirloin steak with salsa verde and rustic roast potatoes 120

homemade stock 185

seared beef salad with crispy onions and horseradish mayonnaise 152

steak and oyster pie 157

Beets: piquant 168

roast stuffed duck with beets 159

soup with chive cream 105

Berries: summer berries with sweet geranium leaves 87

Beurre blanc: with baked sole or flounder and summer herbs 68

panfried scallops with beurre blanc 29

Black pudding: with glazed apples and grainy mustard sauce 154

Black-eyed peas and chickpea stew 160

Black currants: black-currant leaf sorbet 46

see also Berries

Blueberries: carrageen moss pudding with crushed blueberries 88

see also Berries

Bread: Ballymaloe white yeast bread 180

crostini 184

crusty breadsticks 22

foccaccia with caramelized onions, Cashel Blue cheese and walnuts 178

rhubarb bread and butter pudding 46

Swedish flat bread 179

wheaten 176

white soda bread 180

white soda bread with herbs 181

Broccoli 165

Cabbage: spring cabbage soup with crispy seaweed 21

Cakes: almond cake with crystallized violets and angelica 48

candied julienne of lemon peel 189

chocolate caraque 189

Cardamom: yogurt and cardamom mold with pomegranate seeds perfumed with rose water 172

Cardoons layered with Parmesan 38

Carrageen moss pudding with crushed blue-berries 88

Carrot and cumin soup 148

Cauliflower, Romanesco 165

Celery root and apple purée 168

Chanterelles: see Mushrooms

Cheese: cardoons layered with Parmesan 38

carpaccio with slivers of Parmesan, arugula, and truffle oil 23

Cashel Blue cheese foccaccia with caramelized onions and walnuts 178

fresh cheese ravioli with parsley pesto and tomato fondue 155

goat cheese crostini with balsamic onions and watercress 27

homemade cheese with herbs and crackers 94

mozzarella quesadillas with squash blossoms, guacamole, and tomato salsa 62

Parmesan chips 188

poached plums with mascarpone 137

sheep's milk cheese and baby fava beans with olive oil 78

spiced eggplant with goat cheese and arugula leaves 112

stuffed zucchini blossoms with goat cheese, basil, pesto, and tomato fondue 64

Chestnuts see Marrons glacés

Chickpeas: black-eyed peas and chickpea stew 160

spiced chickpea soup 148

Chicken: chicken with morels 34

homemade stock 184

with Jerusalem artichokes 158

tarragon chicken with chile and tomato fondue 123

Thai chicken, galangal, and cilantro soup 150

Chile: Ballycotton shrimps with chile, cilantro, and lemon grass 61

chile and tomato fondue 130

herb and pepper oil 184

hot buttered lobster with chile and cilantro 70oil (Olio Picante) 184

tarragon chicken with chile and tomato fondue 123

Chinese artichokes 168

Chives: beet soup with chive cream 105

fish mousse with chanterelles and chive butter sauce 108

Chocolate: autumn leaves with chocolate mousse 132

caraque 189

cases filled with silky chocolate mousse 171

diamonds with vanilla ice-cream and kumquat compote 173

mousse 132, 171

Cilantro: Ballycotton shrimp with chile, cilantro, and lemon grass 61

cream with crab cakes and salsa cruda 114

hot buttered lobster with chile and cilantro 70

and pea soup 58

Thai chicken, galangal, and cilantro soup 150

Citrus fruit salad 44

Clove jelly 189

Cod: gratin of cod with Imokilly Cheddar and mustard 156

roasted cod with crispy onions and parsley pesto 31

roasted cod with roasted cherry tomatoes and basil oil 71

Corn with marjoram 128

Crab cakes with cilantro cream and salsa cruda 114

Crackers: homemade 94

Cream: Agen prunes stuffed with walnuts and rosewater cream 177

autumn raspberry gelatins with fresh mint cream 136

chive cream 105

cilantro cream with crab cakes and salsa cruda 114

semifreddo di Mandorle 43

spring creams with green gooseberry and elderflower compote 42

Crostini 184

tapenade toasts 186

Crystallized violets: Lydia's almond cake with crystallized violets and angelica 48

Cucumbers: pickled 187

soused herring, pickled cucumbers, and sweet dill mayonnaise 151

Cumin and carrot soup 148

Damson gin 138

Dill: mayonnaise 187

smoked fish with horse-radish mayonnaise and sweet dill mayonnaise 150

soused herring, pickled cucumbers, and sweet dill mayonnaise 151

vinegar 184

Dressings: Ballymaloe vinaigrette 182

basil 80

chargrilled summer vegetables 66

French 182

herb vinaigrette 167

honey and herb 81

lemon oil 109

roasted garlic oil 184

Duck: homemade stock 185

roasted stuffed duck with beets 159

Eels: fresh eel with butter and lemon 69

Eggplant: chargrilled scallops with eggplant and pesto 28

roast pork with spiced eggplant 120

spiced eggplant with goat cheese and arugula leaves 112

Elderflower: sorbet 46

spring creams with green gooseberry and elderflower compote 42

vinegar 184

Fava beans: with olive oil and sheep's milk cheese 78

risotto with fava beans, green peas, asparagus, and sugar snaps 36

Fennel: sea bass with asparagus and fennel 30

Fish: court bouillon 70

fish mousse with chanterelles and chive butter sauce 108

light fish soup with scallions 59

smoked fish with horse-radish mayonnaise and sweet dill mayonnaise 150

Fish see also species

Flounder: baked flounder with melted butter and summer herbs 68

Foccaccia with caramelized onions, Cashel Blue cheese, and walnuts 178

Frittata with oven-roasted tomatoes and summer herbs 74

Fruit salad: citrus 44

Galangal: Thai chicken and cilantro soup 150

Garam masala 72

Garlic: deep-fried sprats with aïoli 24

roasted garlic oil 184

stir-fried zucchini with garlic and ginger 128

whole roasted 83

wild garlic soup 20

Ginger: mushrooms 130

stir-fried zucchini with garlic and ginger 128

Thai chicken, galangal and cilantro soup 150

Globe artichoke bottoms braised in olive oil 84

Goat cheese see Cheese

Gooseberries: spring creams with green gooseberry and elder-flower compote 42

Gravy 35

Guacamole see Avocados

Guineafowl: with Jerusalem artichokes 158

roast guineafowl with parsnip chips and red-currant sauce 118

Haddock: gratin of haddock with Imokilly Cheddar and mustard 156

Hake: gratin of hake with Imokilly Cheddar and mustard 156

roasted hake with crispy onions and parsley pesto 31

roasted hake with roasted cherry tomatoes and basil oil 71

Ham: glazed ham with tomato fondue and scallion champ 122

Hamburgers with ginger mushrooms and buffalo fries 124

Hazelnuts: yogurt with apple blossom honey and toasted hazelnuts 133

Herbs: baked sole or flounder with melted butter and summer herbs 68

clove jelly 189

flavored oils and vinegars 184

frittata with oven-roasted tomatoes and summer herbs 74
herb butter 68
herb dressing 167
herb salad with basil dressing and Parmesan chips 80
homemade cheese with herbs and crackers 94
tisanes 95
white soda bread with herbs 181
Herbs see also individual varieties
Herring: soused herring, pickled cucumbers, and sweet dill mayonnaise 151
Hollandaise sauce 182
with baked sole or flounder and summer herbs 68
wild Irish salmon with seakale 30
Honey: lavender icecream 88
yogurt with apple blossom honey and toasted hazelnuts 133
Horseradish: mustard and horseradish sauce 186
horseradish mayonnaise 186
with seared beef salad and crispy onions 152
with smoked fish and sweet dill mayonnaise 150
with smoked Irish salmon with potato wafers 24

Icecream: Christmas semifreddo with raisins and marrons glacés 170
fraises des bois icecream with strawberry and rhubarb compote 92
fresh lemon icecream with crystallized lemon peel 44
honey lavender 88
pure vanilla icecream with kumquat compote and chocolate diamonds 173
Semifreddo di Mandorle 43

Jellies: herb 189
sweet geranium 189
Jerusalem artichokes with pheasant 158

Kale: buttered kale 39
curly kale and its cousins 165
Kohlrabi with marjoram 84
Kumquat: compote with pure vanilla icecream

and chocolate diamonds 173

Lamb: Easter lamb with roasted scallions 35
Madhur Jaffrey's butterflied leg of lamb 72
tagine of lamb with preserved lemons 162
warm salad of lamb kidneys, straw potatoes, and caramelized shallots 26
Lavender: honey lavender icecream 88
Leek champ 126
Lemon balm 90, 95
Lemon verbena: and lemon balm sorbet 90
tisane 95
Lemon grass: Ballycotton shrimp with chile, cilantro and lemon grass 61
lemonade 95
Lemons: black-currant leaf lemonade 49
candied julienne of lemon peel 189
fresh lemon icecream with crystallized lemon peel 44
lemon-grass lemonade 95
Moroccan preserved lemons 166
tagine of lamb with preserved lemons 162
Lentilles du Puy 131
Lobster: hot buttered lobster with chile and cilantro 70
hot buttered lobster with summer herbs 70
Loganberries: see also Berries
tart or tartlets 92

Mackerel: warm poached mackerel with Bretonne sauce 117
Marjoram: with braised turnips 40
with corn 128
with kohlrabi 84
pattypan squash with marjoram 127
Marrons glacés: Christmas semi-freddo with raisins and 170
Marzipan apple tart 175
Mascarpone see cheese
Mayonnaise: horseradish 152, 186
sweet dill 187
Meringue roulade with summer strawberries and fresh raspberry sauce 91
Mint: autumn raspberry gelatins with fresh mint cream 136

jelly 189
mint and parsley pesto 186
sauce 188
tisane 95
vine-ripened tomato and spearmint soup 60
Morels see Mushrooms
Mullet: Deh-Ta Hsiung's steamed striped mullet 32
striped sea mullet with Cheddar and mustard 156
poached mullet with Hollandaise and pea and parsley champ 116
Mushrooms: chicken with morels 34
dried mushroom oil 184
fish mousse with chanterelles and chive butter sauce 108
ginger 130
hamburgers with ginger mushrooms and buffalo fries 124
pasta with chanterelles, tapenade, and flat-leaf parsley 75
portobella with parsley pesto and balsamic vinegar 111
wild mushroom soup 104
Mustard:
black pudding, with glazed apples and grainy mustard sauce 154
grainy mustard sauce 182
gratin of cod with Imokilly Cheddar and mustard 156
mustard and horse radish sauce 186
Mustard greens 110

Oils: flavored 184
Okra in batter 79
Olives: tapenade 186
Onions: aigre-doux onions with thyme leaves 78
caramelized 164
crispy 188
foccacia with caramelized onions, Cashel Blue cheese, and walnuts 178
goat cheese crostini with balsamic onions and watercress 27
rutabaga with caramelized onions 164
and sage stuffing 159
seared beef salad with crispy onions and horseradish mayonnaise 152

Onions see also Scallions, Shallots
Oranges: blood orange tart 174
citrus fruit salad 44
Oysters: Chez Panisse 109
and steak pie 157

Parmesan see Cheese
Parsley: fresh cheese ravioli with parsley pesto and tomato fondue 155
and mint pesto 186
pasta with chanterelles, tapenade and flat-leaf parsley 75
and pea champ 126
pesto 186
poached striped mullet with Hollandaise and pea and parsley champ 116
portobella mushrooms with parsley pesto and balsamic vinegar 111
Parsnips: chips 127
and potato mash 166
roast guineafowl with parsnip chips and red-currant sauce 118
venison stew with potato and parsnip mash 158
Pasta: with chanterelles, tapenade, and flat-leaf parsley 75
with chargrilled summer vegetables 66
fresh cheese ravioli with parsley pesto and tomato fondue 155
papardelle with roasted pumpkin, pine nuts, and arugula leaves 124
summer pasta with zucchini and sugar snaps 76
Pastry 183
Pattypan squash with basil or marjoram 127
Peaches: peach and raspberry crisp 90
Peas: and cilantro soup 58
and parsley champ 126
poached striped mullet with Hollandaise and pea and parsley champ 116
risotto with fava beans, green peas, asparagus, and sugar snaps 36
summer pasta with zucchini and sugar snaps 76
Peel: candied 189
Pesto: chargrilled scallops with eggplant and pesto 28
with chargrilled summer vegetables 66

fresh cheese ravioli with tomato fondue and parsley 155
mint and parsley 186
parsley 186
portobella mushrooms with balsamic vinegar and parsley 111
stuffed zucchini blossoms with goat cheese, basil, and tomato fondue and 64
Pheasant with Jerusalem artichokes 158
Pickled cucumbers 187
Pine nuts: baby beef scaloppine and spinach with raisins and 73
papardelle with roasted pumpkin, arugula leaves, and 124
with raisins and spinach 82
sweet-sour pork with prunes, raisins, soft polenta, and 160
Piperonata 128
seared tuna with tapenade and 116
Plums: poached plums with mascarpone cheese 137
Polenta 183
sweet-sour pork with prunes, raisins, pine nuts and soft polenta, 160
Pomegranate seeds with rosewater 172
Pork: marinade 160
roast pork with spiced eggplant 120
sweet-sour pork with prunes, raisins, pine nuts, and soft polenta 160
Potatoes: buffalo fries 124
chargrilled sirloin steak with salsa verde and rustic roast potatoes 120
hamburgers with ginger mushrooms and buffalo fries 124
and parsnip mash 166
Pink Fir Apple 130
potato, scallion, and tarragon soup with crusty breadsticks 22
scallion champ 40
smoked Irish salmon with potato wafers and horseradish mayonnaise 24
venison stew with potato and parsnip mash 158
warm salad of lamb kidneys, straw potatoes, and caramelized shallots 26

Praline 43
Prunes: stuffed with walnuts and rosewater cream 177
sweet-sour pork with prunes, raisins, pine nuts, and soft polenta 160
Pumpkin: papardelle with roasted pumpkin, pine nuts, and arugula leaves 124
roasted seeds 106
soup 106

Quesadillas with squash blossoms, mozzarella, guacamole, and tomato salsa 62
Quince paste 138

Radishes with butter, bread, and sea salt 63
Raisins: baby beef scaloppine and spinach with raisins and pine nuts 73
Christmas semifreddo with raisins and marrons glacés 170
with spinach and pine nuts 82
sweet-sour pork with prunes, raisins, pine nuts, and soft polenta 160
Raspberries: autumn raspberry gelatins with fresh mint cream 136
meringue roulade with summer strawberries and fresh raspberry sauce 91
peach and raspberry crisp 90
see also Berries
Red currants: red-currant sauce 187
roast guineafowl with parsnip chips and red-currant sauce 118
see also Berries
Rhubarb: fraises des bois icecream with strawberry and rhubarb compote 92
fresh rhubarb tart 86
rhubarb bread and butter pudding 46
Risotto with fava beans, green peas, asparagus, and sugar snaps 36
Romanesco cauliflower 165
Rosewater with pomegranate seeds 172
Rosemary: jelly 189
oil 184
and spinach soup 58
tisane 95
Rosewater: Agen prunes stuffed with walnuts

191

and rosewater cream
177
Roux 182
Rutabaga with
caramelized onions
164

Sage and onion stuffing
159
Salads: garden herb and
herb flower salad with
basil dressing and
Parmesan chips 80
seared beef salad with
crispy onions and
horseradish
mayonnaise 152
summer garden salad
81
tomato salad 82
warm salad of lamb
kidneys, straw
potatoes, and
caramelized shallots
26
winter green salad with
herb vinaigrette 167
Salmon: smoked Irish
salmon with potato
wafers and horse-
radish mayonnaise 24
with Swiss chard 156
wild Irish salmon with
seakale 30
Salsas: chargrilled sirloin
steak with salsa verde
and rustic roast
potatoes 120
Quesadillas with squash
blossoms, mozzarella,
guacamole, and
tomato salsa 62
Salsa cruda 187
Salsa verde 187
tomato and cilantro
187
Sauces: apple 187
béchamel 182
Bretonne 117

chive butter 108
grainy mustard 182
gravy 35
herb butter 68
Hollandaise 182
mint 188
mustard and
horseradish 186
pesto 186
piperonata 128
raspberry 91
red-currant 187
roux 182
spinach-butter sauce 33
tapenade 186
venison 158
Sausages: winter vegetable
and bean soup with
spicy sausage 149
Scallions: Easter
lamb with roasted
scallions 35
glazed loin of bacon
with tomato fondue
and scallion champ
122
light fish soup with
scallions 59
potato, scallion, and
tarragon soup with
breadsticks 22
Scallion champ 40
Scallops: chargrilled
scallops with eggplant
and pesto 28
panfried scallops with
beurre blanc 29
Scones 181
Sea bass: with asparagus
and fennel 30
Deh-Ta Hsiung's
steamed sea bass 32
roasted sea bass with
roasted cherry
tomatoes and basil oil
71
Seakale: with melted
butter 38
wild Irish salmon with

seakale 30
Semifreddo see Ice cream
Shallots: caramelized 26
see also Onions
Shrimp: Ballycotton
shrimp with chile,
cilantro, and lemon
grass 61
Sloe gin 138
Sole: baked sole with
melted butter and
summer herbs 68
Sorbet: black-currant leaf
46
lemon verbena and
lemon balm 90
Soups: beet with chive
cream 105
carrot and cumin 148
Wild mushroom 104
homemade stocks
184–5
light fish soup with
scallions 59
pea and cilantro 58
pumpkin 106
spiced chickpea 148
spinach and rosemary
58
Spring cabbage with
crispy seaweed 21
Thai chicken, galangal
and cilantro 150
vine-ripened tomato
and spearmint 60
wild garlic 20
winter vegetable and
bean soup with spicy
sausage 149
Spinach: baby beef
scaloppine and
spinach with raisins
and pine nuts 73
baked trout with
spinach-butter sauce
33
with raisins and pine
nuts 82
and rosemary soup 58

Sprats: deep-fried sprats
with aïoli 24
Stocks 184-5
Strawberries: fraises des
bois ice cream with
strawberry and
rhubarb compote 92
meringue roulade with
summer strawberries
and fresh raspberry
sauce 91
see also Berries
Stuffing: sage 159
Sweet geranium: jelly 188
roast woodcock with
sweet geranium jelly
163
summer berries with
sweet geranium leaves
87
tisane 95
Swiss chard: salmon with
swiss chard 156
Syrup for fruit 87, 93

Tapenade 186
chargrilled summer
vegetables with
tapenade toasts 66
pasta with chanterelles,
tapenade, and flat-leaf
parsley 75
seared tuna with
piperonata and 116
Tarragon: chicken with
chile and tomato
fondue 123
potato, scallion, and
tarragon soup with
breadsticks 22
vinegar 184
Tarts: blood orange 174
fresh apricot 86
loganberry 92
marzipan apple 175
walnut tart with
Armagnac 176
Thyme leaves with
aigre-doux onions 78
Vegetables: chargrilled

Tisanes 95
Tomatoes: chile and
tomato fondue 130
and cilantro salsa 187
fresh cheese ravioli
with parsley pesto
and tomato fondue
155
fresh tomato juice 104
frittata with oven-
roasted tomatoes and
summer herbs 74
glazed ham with
tomato fondue and
scallion champ 122
roasted sea bass with
roasted cherry
tomatoes and basil oil
71
stuffed zucchini
blossoms with goat
cheese, basil pesto,
and tomato fondue
64
tarragon chicken with
chile and tomato
fondue 123
tomato fondue 182
tomato purée 182
tomato salad 82
vine-ripened tomato
and spearmint soup
60
Tortilla chips 187
Tortillas see Quesadillas
Trout: baked trout with
spinach-butter sauce
33
Truffle oil: carpaccio
with slivers of
Parmesan, arugula,
and 23
Tuna: seared tuna with
piperonata and
tapenade 116
Turnips: braised turnips
with marjoram 40

Vegetables see also
individual varieties
Venison stew with potato
and parsnip mash
158
Vinegar: flavored 184
goat cheese crostini
with balsamic onions
and watercress 27

Walnuts: foccacia with
caramelized onions,
Cashel Blue cheese,
and walnuts 178
tart with Armagnac
176
Watercress: goat cheese
crostini with balsamic
onions and 27
Woodcock: roast with
sweet geranium jelly
163

Yogurt: with apple
blossom honey and
toasted hazelnuts 133
and cardamom mold
with pomegranate
seeds perfumed with
rosewater 172

Zucchini: stir-fried with
garlic and ginger 128
stuffed zucchini
blossoms with goat
cheese, basil pesto,
and tomato fondue
64
in summer pasta with
sugar snaps 76

summer vegetables
with tapenade toasts
66
homemade stock 185
oven-roasted winter
vegetables 169
winter vegetable and
bean soup with spicy
sausage 149

Roberts Rinehart Publishers Inc.
6309 Monarch Park Place
Niwot, Colorado 80503

ISBN 1-57098-157-4

Text © 1997 Darina Allen
Food photography © 1997 Michelle Garrett
Photography © 1997 Melanie Eclare
Designed by Paul Welti
Typesetting by Peter Howard
Home economy by Fionnuala Ryan and Jane Suthering

Library of Congress 97 068059

Printed and bound in Spain by Mondadori

Photographic acknowledgements

A–Z Botanical Collection: Martin Stankewitz, 20.
Timmy Allen: 2–3; 15; 16 top; 17; 56 bottom. Kevin
Dunne: 102. Melanie Eclare: 1; 4–5; 7–14; 16 bottom;
18 all photos; 19; 24–5; 28 side bar; 29; 30 side bar;
32–3 background; 34; 36 side bar; 50–5; 56 top right;
57; 58 bottom; 72–3; 76 side bar; 78 side bar; 80
bottom; 82; 84–5; 90 side bar; 91; 96–101; 103; 110
bottom; 126; 140–7; 156 side bar; 158 side bar; 166
side bar; 168 side bar. The Garden Picture Library:
Philippe Bonduel, 22. Michelle Garrett: 20–3; 26 side
bar; 28; 31; 32 inset; 35; 37–49; 58 side bar; 59–71;
74–5; 77; 79; 80 side bar; 82–3; 86–9; 90 bottom;
92–5; 104–9; 110 side bar; 111–125; 129–139;
148–155; 156 top; 157–165; 167; 169–181.